_____ 님께

SANG-OK

SHIM'S

POETRY

Again,

B.C.

Sang-Ok Shim's collection of poems

Again, B.C.

다시, 기원전

Written by Sang-Ok Shim
Translated by Eechae Ra

 시인의 말

속셈 없는 외로움처럼
삶을 두근거리게 한다
생각과 부딪치는 두 개의 작용
예기치 못한 것이 만들어지는 나의 세계
시를 쓰면서 편안함을 얻었다
나는 날마다
멀리 갈 수 있다

2021년 새봄

심 상 옥

The Poet's Remarks

Like loneliness that comes from lack of intention,
It makes my life flutter:
Those two actions collide with my thoughts.
It's my world where unexpected things are made.
I gained comfort by writing poems.
I can go far away every day.

Early Spring 2020

Sang-Ok Shim

차례 Contents

차례 Contents

2. 나의 세계는 권태에서 시작한다
My World Begins With Boredom

차례 Contents

3. 다시 기원전
Again, B.C

차례 Contents

4. 신들의 이야기
The Story of the Gods

차례 Contents

5. 일상속의 날카로움
   The Sharpness of Daily Life

차례 Contents

SANG-OK

SHIM'S

POETRY

PART 1

인간 외적 인간이 온다
More Than Human
Is Coming

유현미의 세계

내 마음결도 청자라면 좋겠다
살결이 동방의 사파이어라
중국 본고장 정촉진 도요지 바닥에 널려있지만
유현미의 세계 바로 그 자체이다
네댓 걸음만 걸어도 노점 널빤지 위에
펼쳐진 이싱 정촉진의 사파이어
너를 생각하지 않고는 천년의 긴 여름
내 그리움에도 청자 같은 환상의 세계가 있으면 좋겠다
창살을 누를 때마다
환상은 구름처럼 피어나고
너를 잊지 않고는 천년의 긴 겨울
마지막으로
네 환상의 세계를 이룬 이미지를 그렸을 때
내가 만든 창살은
환상의 세계가 아니라
청자 같은 느낌의 긴 그리움이었다

The Immeasurable Deep and Exquisite Beauty World

I wish I had a celadon heart,

Whose skin is the sapphire of the East.

Even if it is on the ground of Jiangsu Province,

China's home town of the kiln site;

It's a world itself of immeasurable deep and

exquisite beauty.

Lots of sapphire of Yixing spreads out on the stall boards

Every three or four steps.

A thousand years of long summer without thinking of you;

I wish there was a world of fantasy like the celadon

in my longing.

Every time I press the plaid patterns,

Fantasy blooms like clouds;

A thousand years of long winter without forgetting you:

At last

When the image of your fantasy world was born,

The plaid patterns I made,

Beyond the fantasy world,

Have become a long longing of a celadon.

실험적 산물

옛것에서부터
강렬한 색채에 이르기까지
소재는 수없이 많지
꽃을 심고
데생을 하고
합창 교향곡을 작곡하고
나라를 세울 수도 있지
실험적 산물을 찾아 예술을 떠날 수도 있지
원색감각으로 대상의 클로즈업을 할 수도 있지
화신도 권태를 이기지 못해
흙으로 공간을 결합하여
윤기 나는 화려함과 추상적
색채가 이국적 분위기를 자아내는
세상에서 가장 현대적인 감각이 연출된
실험적 산물을 만들었다네

Experimental Products

From the old things

To the fullness of colors

There's a lot of material:

You can

Plant flowers,

Make a sketch,

Write a choral symphony,

Build a country

Leave art in search of experimental products, or

Zoom in on objects with primary colors.

The god of fire couldn't overcome boredom and

Produce experimental products

Combining space with soil

To create the most modern sensations of the world

With its glossy splendor and

Abstract colors.

창조의 시간

풍요로운 정감의 힘이
한 덩이의 내적 세계가
나를 움직인다
잊혀진 것 보다
버림받고 내던져진 것이
무한의 풍요로 움직인다
너는 어째서
날마다
나를 움직여 영원을 추구하게 하느냐
여전히
상상 속의 제작에 볼륨을 주고
여전히
잠재적인 조형미를 티끌에서 부르게 하고
여전히
나의 형체를 만들어 가는 고통을 안기느냐
너는 어째서
날마다 이토록 만들어가며
창밖의 한 줌 흙이 아닌
속삭임의 새 순으로 만들어 버리느냐
고뇌 너머 기쁨을 빚느냐

Creation Time

The power of a rich feeling and

The whole inner world

Moves me.

The abandoned things rather than

The unremembered

Act as an infinite abundance.

Why do you

Move me

Day after day

To pursue eternity;

Still

Give volume

To imaginative production;

Still

Have potential formative beauty call from the dust;

Still

Give me the pain of making my shape?

Why do you make every day

New whispering buds

Not a handful of earth outside the window?

Do you create joy over anguish?

그릇의 모양새

무기적인 소재에 잎이 돋아났다
가슴이 뻐근해졌다
무기적인 소재가 만들어내는 기묘한 시도 속에
가마 앞에 혼자 있는 기분
야릇한 존재감이 느껴졌다
화신火神은 왜
심미안과 창조적인 자기 목표를
세울 수 없다는 생각을 했을까
없는 듯 있는
흙이 가지고 있는 가능성과 그 잠재력인 세계에
순수한 마음을 등에 지고
새로운 형태의 조형물이 무성하게
허공에 퍼져있다
전통도예가 지닌 아름다움이 아니라
그릇의 모양새에 이끌렸다
잠재된 조형미는 흙이
말하지 않는 또 다른 말이다
비로소 새로운 발견이 이루어지는 순간이다

The Shape of Pottery

Leaves sprouted from inorganic material.

My heart was full.

Trying to give quaintness to the inorganic material,

I feel alone in front of the kiln and

It even gives me a strange presence.

Why did the god of fire think that

Man could not set his own creative goals

With the aesthetic?

Seemingly nonexistent but existent earth,

On the back of the pure heart of the world of

Which with possibility and potential,

New forms of sculpture are scattered

In the air.

I was attracted to the shape of pottery

Rather than the beauty of traditional ones.

The latent formative beauty is another word that

Was not said by the earth:

That is the moment when a new discovery is made.

흙을 빚으면서

넌 본디 별이었다
티끌로 부서졌다 다시 뭉쳐질 수밖에 없는
태고로부터 숨을 불어 넣은 비술의 우주
태워져서 찬란히 빛나는 자태로
찰라에 잉태되는 도예의 심연에
불꽃으로 산화한 생명의 상징이 너라는 것
나는 너를 누르고 구부리고
찌그러뜨리고 구멍을 뚫어
변형법을 시도한다
회색에 회색을 덧칠하는 것이 이론의 모든 것
오직 살아있는 것은
전통도자기에 대한 반발이다

While Fashioning an Earthenware

Earth, you were naturally a star,

The universe born by secret methods that

Breathed from ancient times,

Broken into dust and then gotten together again.

You are the symbol of life that has been oxidized

to flames

From the abyss of pottery that

Is burned and born in a flash into a shining figure.

By pressing you, bending,

Crushing, and drilling,

I try to transform.

To paint gray with gray is all in theory, and

Only a reaction to tradition is proof it is alive.

흙과 인간

도자기는 음악이나 자연과
가까운 관계이다
스스로를 속이지 않겠다는
마음을 가지려고 흙을 보았다
그런데 사람 손에 의해서 만들어진
작품을 만들지 않으려고
더 큰 자연에 길들지 않았다
나는 낙오되어야 살아남는다는
뚜어뚜어의 말을 믿었다
실험적인 도자기를 빚으려고
흙을 절단 내었다
절단 내어야 도자기가
자극을 받는 까닭이다
도자기를 만드는 과정에서 기교가
표면에 나타나지 않아야 살아남는다는
화신의 말도 믿었다
그 속에 흙과 인간의 끝없는 관계
신비함이 마음을 움직인다

Earth and Man

Pottery is closely related to

Music and nature.

When I tried not to deceive myself,

I met the earth.

And I tried not to tame the larger nature

So as not to make a work

Made by human hands.

I cut up the soil

To make experimental pottery,

Remembering Duoduo's saying that

Man could survive if he failed

Because cutting the pottery

Will motivate it.

I also believed in the words of the god of fire that

I would survive only

If techniques did not appear on the surface

In the process of making pottery.

The mystery of the endless relationship

Between earth and man moves my heart.

한 잔의 차

1976년 대만 T. TV에 출연하여
한국도예에 대해 말하려다
나는 한 잔의 차에 대해 말하고 말았다
꽃은 우울과 불안을 한 방에 날려 버리는데
저를 시들게 하는 가뭄에도
꽃을 피운다고 한다
그 꽃의 다른 이름이 한 잔의 차이다
꽃은 쉴 새 없이 개성적이지
꽃이 언제 우는 것 보았느냐
네 웃음도
저 꽃에서 시작되었으면 좋겠다
차도 슬픈 이별의 감정마저
마중이 필요할지 몰라
이제부터
한 잔의 차는
속된 세상의 때와 권태
그리고 이별의 감정마저 깨끗이 씻어 내는 것이다

A Cup of Tea

When I appeared on Taiwan's T. TV in 1976,

I was going to talk about Korean porcelain,

But I ended up talking about a cup of tea.

Flowers that blow away depression and anxiety

in one shot

Bloom even in the drought that

Withers them.

Another name for the flower is a cup of tea.

Flowers are constantly unique.

By the way, have you ever seen a flower cry?

I hope your smile begins

With that flower.

You might need a cup of tea

To meet your sad parting.

From now on

A cup of tea cleans up the filth of

The vulgar world, boredom,

And parting feelings.

파리에서 일본 토우를 만나다

파리의 길가
카페의 테라스에 주인이 없다
파리장들이 스마트한 옷차림이 되어
떠나가는 나그네가 있을 뿐
허무한 눈으로
방심한 표정으로
지친 일본 토우의 눈이여
한동안 바라보았다
다른 익살스런 얼굴을 버리고 어디든 간다
다시 돌아온 길을 지우고 가는 바람 소리
백 년 전 조수 모양을 한 시멘트 악귀도 제길로 돌아가고
문득 돌아보니
구석구석 서 있다
갈 길 얻지 못한 몸
나를 이미 웃고 있는 얼굴로 만들었구나

Meeting Japanese Clay Figurines in Paris

There is no owner on the terrace of the cafe

By the roadside in Paris;

There are only people who leave

Like travelers in smart Paris Jeans.

I looked at the tired Japanese clay figurines

With empty eyes and

A careless look

For a while.

The wind that erases the way back

With a comical look on its face;

Looking around there,

I saw the hundred years old cement demons

Shaped like birds and beasts, leaving

After standing in every corner by corner.

Even if they don't have a way to go,

They made me laugh already!

흙과 인체의 통일성

흙의 매력 가운데 하나는
그에게 있는 아름다운 침묵이다

인체의 매력 가운데 하나는
그에게 있는 원초적 상태의 침묵이다

소유하는 것이 사랑은 아니다

자연의 모든 생명체보다 더 희생 같은 사랑
그것이 살아가는 생명력의 침묵이다

Uniformity of Earth and Human Body

One of the charms of earth
Is its beautiful silence.

One of the attractions of the human body
Is the silence of the primitive state in it.

To own is not to love

Love is like the sacrifice of all life in nature:
That is the silence of the vitality of life.

인간 외적 인간이 온다

9회째 개인 도예전을 열면서
그 햇수만큼 나이를 먹지만
신비한 표정을 한
도예를 한 점을 얻었을 때
그냥 좋아서
한 끼 밥 안 먹어도
배고프지 않네
어쩌다가 도자기를 만들기에
창문처럼 구멍이 뚫린 곳으로
화신이 온다고 했듯이
흙을 빚고 있는 나에게 가기 모습을 달리함에 엉기면
작품 외적 작품이 나온다고 소리칠 텐데
그릇을 빚어 말렸다가
애벌구이한 후 유약을 칠한다
가끔 실망을 안겨 주는 모든 경우마저
기쁨을 안겨 준다
심술이 나서 변덕을 부린 것이나
의도치 않았던 작품이 나오는 것이다
그 끝에서
나의 일생을 담은 너를 기다린다
인간 외적 인간은 내 생각이 담은 그대로 나타난다

More Than Human Is Coming

Even though I'm as old as the number of years
I've been hosting my own pottery exhibition nine times,
When I got a piece of pottery
With a mysterious look,
I'm not hungry
Even if I don't eat a meal
Because I like it.
What led me to make pottery?
When I'm making the soil,
Does the god of fire appear in a window-like hole,
And yell at me that
There's more than work coming out of it?
When I make pottery, dry them,
Do a biscuit firing, and glaze them,
Even though some works may not satisfy me,
They still bring me joy.
Sometimes when they're so mean and fickle,
As long as they are born as unintended works,
I wait for them to capture my life at the end
Until the time when
More than human comes out of my heart.

SANG-OK

SHIM'S

POETRY

PART 2

나의 세계는 권태에서 시작한다
My World Begins
with Boredom

원시인의 신비

원시인 그림하면 생각난다
강변 모래톱에 찍힌
이집트 상형문자 같은
공룡들의 발자국
원시인하면 또 생각난다
수수께끼에 싸인 저녁노을 아래
종이배 접어 띄우며
주술을 외우던
원시인의 의식하면 다시 생각난다
대나무 소리 물새 소리
시간과 공간이 먼저
옮겨 적은 부정의의 대상들
아, 원시인이여 너는
자꾸 내게로 오는 구나
부정됨으로써 소멸되고
실재성을 인정하던 시절
자연 속에 살면서도 부단히
자연과의 투쟁을 벌이던
원시인들이 나를 끌어당긴다

The Mysteries of Primitive Men

One thing that comes to mind
When I think of primitive paintings is
The footprints of dinosaurs,
Such as Egyptian hieroglyphics,
On the sandbar along the river.
Another thing that comes to mind
When I think of primitive paintings is
The spell they used to recite
As they folded and floated a paper boat
Under the mysterious, veiled sunset,
Another things that come to mind
When I think of primitive paintings are
The sounds of bamboo and water birds:
Indeterminate objects
Of which time and space moved first.
Oh, primitive men, you
Keep coming to me
Destroyed by denial,
Acknowledged the reality,
But constantly fought against nature
While living in nature, attract me.

시간을 담은 흙

시간마다 선이 원에서 출발이라는 사람이 있고
흙마다 그릇과 같은 원형이라는 사람도 있는데
봄은 정방형을 움직이게 하는 달이라고 그들은 말하네
여름은 생명의 리듬이 숨 쉬게 하는 달이라고 말하네
흙 앞에 서면
점이나 선으로 이루는 사람이 있고
작품을 이룩하는 사람은
시간을 담은 흙이라고 말하네
과거는 추상적 세계의 경계선을 넘는 사람도 있는데
미래는 자연의 생명력과 질서를 이룬다는 사람이 있고
나는 대체로 점이나 선으로 이룬다

Earth Containing Time

The line is said to be started from the circle;

Earth is called a circle, like a bowl;

Spring is called to move the square;

Summer is also said to be the season

When life rhythmizes and breathes.

People who start with dots or lines

With earth and

Make their work, say that

Earth contains time.

Some say the past crosses the border of

the abstract world,

Some say the future brings natural vitality and order.

I usually achieve by dots or lines.

나의 세계는 권태에서 시작한다

영혼을 추구하며 단 하루만이라도
TV를 끄고
인터넷을 접고
역사의 발자취를 더듬는
울창한 숲길을 찾아서 떠난다면
처음에
햇빛과 바람과 물과 새소리만으로
하루를 채울 수 있다면
나의 세계는 권태에서 시작한다
틈만 나면 데생하고
틈만 나면 이미지가 만들어지는 과정을 보고
다람쥐와 나뭇잎과 별만으로
나만의 이미지로 만든다면
그곳에 내가 두고 온
흙으로부터 속삭임을 들을 수 있을까
들리지 않는 듯 들리는
낯선 소리 들을 수 있을까
흙으로부터 시작하는 나의 세계
여기에
생각과 부딪치는 두 개의 작용
예기치 못한 것이 만들어지는 나의 세계

My World Begins with Boredom

If I turn off the TV,

Close off the Internet,

Trace the footsteps of history, and

Leave to find a dense forest path

In pursuit of my soul,

As we did for the first time,

So I can fill the day with

Only sunlight, wind, water, and birds' song.

My world begins with boredom.

I make images whenever I have time,

And I draw them.

If I make squirrels, leaves, stars, and

The moon my own image,

Can I hear the whisper of the earth

I left behind

From it?

Can I hear the fresh sound

That sounds like I can't hear it?

My world, starting from the soil:

Here the two actions that ideas collide with;

My world where unexpected things are made.

나눔의 시간들

모스크바 강변에 드리워진 그림자가 아름답다
어제보다 나은 오늘이
나와 함께 나눔의 시간을 갖자고 한다
어제는
강에 비친 많은 일화속의 그림자들이
이제는
남 보란 듯 말고
나 보란 듯 살라고 속삭인다
오늘보다 나은 내일이
나와 함께 나눔의 시간을 갖자고 한다
오늘은
펼쳐진 분홍빛 하늘이
내일처럼 살라고
내게 속삭인다
그리고 아주 오랜 시간이 흐른 다음
강은 거대하고 끝이 없으며
하늘처럼 넓어 보이며
나를 끌어당기리
언젠가 너는
평면 속에서
미래의 내 이미지를 드러낸 적 있다

Times of Sharing

The shadow hanging over the Moscow River is beautiful.

Today, which is better than yesterday,

Encourages me to have a time of sharing with it.

The shadows of many anecdotes

In yesterday's river

Whisper to me not to live a life good to others

Anymore,

But to live a life that is good to me.

Tomorrow, which is better than today,

Suggests me to have a time of sharing with it.

The open pink sky

Of today

Whispers to me

To live like tomorrow.

And after a very long time,

The river looks huge, endless,

Wide like the sky and

Pulls me.

One day, you

Revealed my image of the future

Even in the plane.

끊임없는 설레임

구운 도자기를 끄집어낼 때는
착잡한 심정이 엇갈린다
태깔이 멋지고 모양도 빚은 그대로
나오는 것이 있는가 하면
공허한 인간의 말보다
폐허 속의 한 포기 풀이 아름답다고 말해도 될까
빛깔이 바래고 주저앉아서
보기 흉한 몰골이 돼 있는 것도 있다
두 개가 서로 엉겨 붙어 있는가 하면
터져서 금이 가버린 것도 있다
그런데 불의 장난이라고 할까
가장 척박한 곳에서 자라난
생명나무는 바로 웃음이라고 해도 될까
참으로 신묘해 보이는 것도 있다
생각조차 하지 못했던 결과치고는
끊임없는 설레임도 안겨줄까

Ceaseless Excitement

Whenever I take out the baked pottery,

I have mixed feelings.

Some appear nice in shape and color,

And they are the way I expected,

On the other hand, some appear

As if they were empty human words

Or grasses in the ruins, faded in color and

Collapsed to look ugly.

There are cases where the two are intertwined,

Some of them burst and cracked.

Is this all a trick of fire?

Isn't the life tree smiling that bloomed

In the most barren place?

Do some look really

Strange and unexpected

Give me a constant thrill?

검은 신들

나고야에서 지하철로 40분 가면
일본의 전통도요지로 400년 역사를
지닌 세도지방이다
도자기를 만들 때
손은 연장 중의 연장이다
흙을 만질 때마다
왼손의 온기가
오른손으로 번진다
흙 한 점
물 한 방울
불타는 소리
1971년, 오리베기법을 배울 때 나는
아무것도 바라지 않는다
아무것도 두려워하지 않는다
백절불굴의 의지가
가마에서 불탄다
수십 개의 자기가 빛나도
반드시 크게 돋보이는 것이 있다
나는 계속
형 누르기와 동으로 발색하는 녹색
붉은색의 유약을 잘 쓸 생각이라고

무기적 소재를 시도하고
창조적인 자기 세계가 요구된다
나는 떠오른 해를 두고
검은 신들께 기원할 생각이다

Black Gods

If you go 40 minutes by subway from Nagoya,
You will find Seto City, which has 400 years of history
For traditional Japanese pottery.
When you make pottery,
Your hand is one of the tools.
Every time I touch clay,
The warmth of my left hand
Spreads to my right hand.
A piece of clay,
A drop of water, and
The sound of burning.
In 1971, when I learned Oribe techniques,
I didn't want anything,
I wasn't afraid of anything, and
My indomitable will was burning
In the kiln.
Among the dozens of shiny ceramics,
There must be something that stands out.
I think I will continue pressing the shape,
Using the green and red glaze that
Comes out of the copper,

Trying the inorganic material, and

I will pray to the black gods

As I see the rising sun

To realize my creative self-realization.

평면으로 한 입체

들풀에 이름을 지어주고 싶은 마음이
흙을 살아가게 했다고 흙은 말한다
어느 사이 흙이 분분하게
흩어져 버려질 때
어제와 같은 오늘을
살지 않겠다고 다짐하던 날들이
흙에게는 있었다
20년 전에 오사카 시립박물관은
비디오테이프를 사용한 작품들이 전시되었다
대체로 '평면'과 '입체'를 볼 수 있다
편화는 회화와 닮았지만
중력이 되는 점이 다르다
중력을 합한다고 하는 것은
수직 방향을 취하지 않고
기운 방향으로 향한다
이로써 수평과 수직의 짜임새가 이루어진다
시련의 끝에서 보면
그 공간의 여백이라는 평면은
반입체에서 태어났다고 한다

Planes Born from Isometric Structure

Earth says that the desire to name the grass

Has kept it alive.

When earth gets scattered

In different ways,

It vows not to live today

Like yesterday.

Twenty years ago, the Osaka Municipal Museum displayed

Works using videotapes.

They generally showed that 'plane' and 'dimensional'

Stylization resembles painting,

But the difference is that the former make you feel

gravity.

When gravity is said to be joining,

It's not taking a vertical direction,

But it's heading in a tilted direction.

This creates a horizontal and vertical arrangement.

At the end of the ordeal,

It is said that a plane called the margin of space was

Born from isometric structure.

화공간花空間의 순간

따뜻한 오후 한나절
나고야 일전회日展會 도예가 가또오
초청으로 차 대접받는 순간에
우주 속에서 으뜸가는 생명의 상징이 있고
다화라는 꽃이 있다고
누가 놀라운 말을 하고
꽃으로 탄생을 가능케 하는 모태이기에
또 누가 놀라운 말을 하지만
나에게는
이 다화를 사랑하는 것에 놀라울 것이 없으니
일본 처녀들은 시집가기 전
반드시 다도를 익힌다고
누가 다시 말차末茶라는 새로운 차도
모르는 생활 묻지 말라
화공간에 놓인 다병을 바라보며
또 누가 다시 새로운 공간을 말하지만
나에게는
대수롭지 않은 만남에서
오고 간 점이 있다고 하듯이
오랜 세월을 두고 잊혀 지지 않기에
시시각각으로 신선미 자꾸 내게로 오는 구나

A Moment in the Flower Space

A warm afternoon

At the tea reception of

A Japanese Nagoya Exhibition ceramist, Gatto.

One participant said remarkable words that

There is a flower in the universe called the symbol of life,

'Da-hwa,' tea flower;

Another participant said that a flower is a maternal belly.

Their remarks were not surprising for me

Who knew that

Japanese girls must learn the tea ceremony

Before marriage.

Again, a person insisted that you should not talk to people

Who don't know 'green tea latte'.

Looking at the many tea pots in the flower space,

Someone else talked about 'a new flower space'.

But what I was thinking was

Love comes and goes

In a trifling encounter.

They are not forgotten for a long time,

But rather come to be fresh from time to time.

현실을 넘어서

베를린 장벽의 붕괴
냉전을 종식한 오늘날에도
세계는 밀접하게 다가서고 있다
한 송이 말 속에서 세상을 읽고
한 그루 사람에게서 오늘을 보듯이
세계화 시대에는
인터넷으로 달려간다
오늘을 보고 시를 읽으면서
전 세계에 자본주의가 전파되듯이
독특한 문화와 기술의 향연이 펼쳐진다
지름이 50센티의 접시들로 이루어진
'현실을 넘어서'라는 주제의 1982년도 도예전이다
나는 날마다
새롭게 흙을 배우는 도예인이 되어
다른 날을 꿈꾼다

Beyond Reality

Since the fall of the Berlin Wall and

The end of the Cold War,

The world is getting closer today.

Unlike the days when

People read the world in a single word

And saw a day in a single person,

In this global age, they run to the Internet.

In it, when they see today and read poetry,

Capitalism spreads all over the world, and

A feast of unique culture and technology unfolds.

The 1982 Pottery Exhibition under the theme "Beyond
Reality,"

Which was composed of plates 50 centimeters in diameter,

Feels a long way off.

But today I still dream

Of another day

As a new potter learning earth.

하루의 즐거운 휴식

중국 강서성에는 신기하게 생긴 동굴
선권동善券洞이라는 경치가 화려한 곳이다
예부터 이름난 시인 묵객들이
기묘함을 읊었던 이곳은
푸른 송백나무로 숲을 이룬 사이로
사람 같기도 한 검은 상들이 다가 온다
남녀의 성기 같은 모양이
용트림하는가 하면
생명체에게 공급하는 탯줄이 다가 온다
모두가 나름의 볼륨이 있으며
모두가 화려한 색상이다
선권동의 기묘한 동굴 속에서
마음을 움직이게 하는 힘이 샘솟고
생각들은 불꽃처럼 부딪치며
하루의 즐거운 휴식을 만끽한다

A Pleasant Break of a Day

In Jiangxi Sheng, China, there is a beautiful scenic spot
Called Shan Juan Cave.
Here, famous poets and painters have long recited
About its wonder,
There are human-like black figures standing
Between the green pine forests.
Men's and women's genitals-like images let out big burps;
Something like the umbilical cord that nourishes life
Unfolds before your eyes.
Everything boasts its own volume
And colorfulness.
In the strange Shan Juan Cave,
The power to move my mind springs up,
My thoughts collide like fireworks,
But I enjoy a pleasant break of a day.

SANG-OK

SHIM'S

POETRY

PART 3

다시, 기원전
Again, B.C.

조용한 그 곳에

줄기로부터 다시 가지와 개화에
꽃을 피우는 가지들
자연은 나에게
존재 이상의 가치를 제공하듯이
인연과 이별을 전해 주며
지난날과 다가올 미래
음미하는 건
무한한 공간과 여유를 주는 시간도 있을 거야
전위작품을 추구하고
도예가 테시가하라 히로시
서로 연결된 통일성 가운데
한 쌍이 이루어내는 삶처럼
'조용한 그곳에' 생명의 리듬이 숨 쉰다
그의 다병은 또
도전정신을 드러내며
구멍이 뚫리고 벌어진 채로
평면에서 공간으로
환상에서 공간으로
서로 반응하면서 공간을 채운다

In That Quiet Place

Like the branches that bloom
With energy from their stems,
Nature, in partnership with me,
Provides more value than existence,
Delivers ties and farewells, and
Connects the past with the future.
Likewise, the rhythm of life is hidden
'In That Quiet Place,' like a pair of lives,
Within the unity of Hiroshi Teshigahara, an artist
Who pursues the avant-garde work
By putting the tea pots to good use
That provides infinite space and room.
To him, the tea pots are also an expression of
The spirit of challenge,
With holes or open,
From plane to space, and
From fantasy to space
They react to each other and fill the space.

이어지는 환상

1981년, 늦은 가을
동경 초월화랑에서 도예 5인전
얼굴같은 형상으로 만든 도조작품이다
낙엽이 바람에 뒹굴고 있다
뒹구는 낙엽 위에 비가 내린다
초월회관 한복판이
다 젖고 있다
나를 흙속으로
들어가게 하는 까닭에
이어지는 환상에도
예기치 못한 것이 만들어 진다
얼굴을 만들어 가는 과정에서
흙으로부터 속삭임을 듣게 되고
여기에
나 자신의 생각과 부딪치는
두 개의 작용이 있어
고뇌와 기쁨이 함께 따른다
이어지는 환상에도 돌출 부위들은
나의 마음을 흔들고 있다
살아있는 듯한 요사스러움도
화려한 색으로 담겨 있다

A Succession of Fantasies

Late autumn, 1981,

Five artists display their face-shaped pottery works

At Chowol Gallery in Tokyo.

The leaves are rolling in the wind;

It rains on the fallen leaves;

The center of the Chowol building

Is all wet.

The soil always

Beckons to me.

And like a succession of fantasies

It gives me unexpected things.

In the process of making faces,

I hear the whispering of the earth,

On top of that,

There are two effects on me

Bumping into my own thoughts,

Which come with agony and joy.

The protruding parts of the fantasy series

Are shaking my mind, the life-like craftiness,

And splendor intersect.

시간의 흐름 속에서

일본의 도코노마는
우리네 벽장과 같은 구실이다
이곳에
그 집안의 전통적인 서화가 담긴 족자
그 밑에 다화茶花가 놓여진다
차 의식에 참여하는 다병茶瓶은
꽃을 받드는 마음에
조형의 오묘함을 찬미하고
자연의 혜택에 감사한다
이곳에
꽃을 소재로 삼은
미의 세계가 창조된다
시간의 흐름이여
다병이여
너를 탐한 40년 동안
너에게 나는
점차 서정적 방향으로 기울어 간다
시간의 흐름 속에서 고정 개념을 지니고
가장 강력하게 살았다고
말해 주마

In the Course of Time

Dokonoma in Japan is

Like a closet in our country.

There's a traditional family painting on the wall,

And underneath, there is a porcelain vase.

Looking at the heart of the tea pot

That supports the flowers in tea ceremonies,

People praise the subtlety of sculpture and

Appreciate the benefits of nature.

Here

A world of beauty is created

With flowers as the subject.

Oh, the flow of time,

Tea pots,

For 40 years I've been wanting you,

I'm gradually leaning towards you

In a lyrical manner.

I'll tell you I've lived

The most powerful life

With fixed concepts in the course of time.

다시, 기원전

동양적 기본형태 위에
현대적 기법과 감각을 조화시킨
기하학적인 선이 시샘을 하나
가마 앞에서 중얼거리다
하루가 다 갔다
나이 들어 바뀐 것은
아버지를 쇠연금술사라 부르고 싶은 마음이
예사롭지 않다는 것이다
기원전은
때 묻지 않은 순수한 달이라고
일본 전통도자기인 오리베 기법에도
나와 함께 해온
오랜 전통도자기에도
제각기 시대의 우수성을 지니고 있다
'다시, 기원전'만한
화신의 세상은 없다
이러한 점토에 공간과 조화를 이루는 것을
테마로 삼는다면
화신만한 미지의 세계에 도전할 수 있다고
즐거움도 숨을 쉴 수 있겠다

Again, B.C.

I spent the whole day

Muttering in front of the kiln,

Wondering if the geometric line

Harmonizing modern techniques and senses

On top of the basic oriental form was jealous.

What changed with my age was that

I wanted to call my father

An iron alchemist.

The Japanese traditional pottery,

Oribe techniques, that come to mind

When you think that B.C. is

Like a pure moon without dirt, and

The traditional pottery that has been with me,

Also show the excellence of each era.

There would be no other world of the fire god

Like 'Again, B.C.'

If you use clay to create harmony

With space as the theme,

You can challenge the uncharted world of the fire god

And have a place to breathe.

내가 비로소

괴테의 고향인 프랑크푸르트에서
무슨 사색에 잠긴 듯한 표정으로
로렐라이 바위
별로 가보고 싶지 않은
신성로마 황제의 대관식에
수많은 고성과 펼쳐진 포도밭
요정이 뱃사공을 불러
죽게 했다는 이야기에도 허기가 지네
허기가 진다는 건 후회가 많다는 것
강 양편에는
웃고 싶어 하는 바위에 이르기까지
성벽이 있네
내게 진정
무서운 것은 뱃사공
이야기에 슬퍼도 허기가 지네
허기가 지지 않는다는 건
힘이 된다는 것
바로크 건축에 내려앉은 선한
가을빛 아래
녹색 짙은 수목들이
자꾸만 올려다보고 싶어하는 그 모습이

어딘가 소박함을 느끼게 한다
로렐라이의 노래가
사람의 마음을 휘어잡는 것 같이
비로소 알게 되었다

For the First Time, I

The rock of Lorelai
With a contemplative expression on its face
Is in Goethe's hometown of Frankfurt;
The coronation of the Holy Roman Emperor,
Where I do not want to go;
Numerous old castles and open vineyards…
I'm hungry to hear that
The fairy seduced the sailors to death.
Hunger means I have a lot of regrets.
On both sides of the river
There's a wall that stretches to the rock
That wants to laugh.
The real fear for me is that
I feel hungry
For the sad stories of the boatmen.
If you're not hungry,
You're proof that you have power.
Under the good autumn tints
Beating on the Baroque architectures,
The dark green trees that
Make me want to keep looking up,

Make me feel something simple.

For the first time, I realized what

Lorelai's song meant

To win people's hearts.

인어공주 도조상

코펜하겐의 티볼리공원
예부터 문화의 중심지이다
무성한 가로수가 선 아름다운 길을
넘어서 달렸나 보다
안데르센의 나라를 지나쳐버리다니
소를 탄 여신 게피온이
넓게 펼쳐진 바닷가에 주인공이 되어
언제나
슬픈 듯이 바다를 바라보고 있다
흙으로 빚어내는 도자기작업도
흙이 가지고 있는 가능성과
그 잠재적인 세계에 순수한 마음이
가 닿을 때 비로소
새로운 형태의 조형물이 탄생한다

The Mermaid Statue

The Tivoli Garden in Copenhagen

Has long been a cultural center.

I must have run too much

Along the beautiful street with trees

To pass Andersen's country.

Goddess Gefjon riding a cow

Always

Looks at the sea sadly

As if she is the main character on a wide beach.

The work of pottery produced from the soil

Is only created

When a pure heart touches

The possibility of the soil and

Its potential world.

너와 함께라면

도예는 비록 비틀어진 물체일지라도
저마다 아름다운 특성을 갖고 있고
보잘것없는 것들 속에도 화신이 숨어 있다
형태와 무늬가 단순한 흐름으로 이어진 작품에도
운치가 있고
철사와 남색이 조합하여 묘한 리듬을 그린다
너와 함께라면 실용과 이상이 함께 휘돌아 흐른다
또한 화신은 나를 영원히 취하게 한다

If I Am with You

Even though it's a twisted object,

Each pottery has its own beautiful characteristics,

The god of fire is hidden among the humble.

There is a sense of beauty in works where

Shapes and patterns lead to simple flows.

A combination of wire and

Navy brings out a strange rhythm.

When I'm with you,

Practicality and ideals run together.

Also, the god of fire makes me drunk forever.

흔적

속을 파낸 거목 몇 그루
덩굴에 매달려 큰 발에 엉켜 있다
한 가지에 꽃이 너무 많이 피면
꽃솎음을 해야 한다기에
봄이 어느 사이 성큼 다가와
자연에서 얻은 감동 애정으로 이어지는데
나의 흔적은 하나같이
상처가 난 알몸이었고
속이 파여 있다
몸체는 창살과 같은 구멍이 뚫려 있다
각기 모습을 달리하여
거꾸로 하거나 매달려 있기도 하다
그렇지만 상호 조합되면서
새로운 느낌을 보이기도 한다
이때 내 마음은 더욱 흙에게
가까워지는 듯하다

Trace

Some of the giant trees that have been hollowed out
Are entangled in a net and hung from the vines.
Spring is coming,
So if there are too many flowers on one branch,
Some flowers must be cut out.
The emotions I get from nature lead to affection,
But my traces are
All damaged naked
And hollow.
There are arrow-shaped holes in my body.
They are either upside down or hanging
In different shapes.
But they can also be combined
To show a new feeling.
At this point, my mind
Seems to be getting closer to earth.

현대를 사는 인간

꽃의 조형미를 칭송하고
자연의 아름다움에 취해
하늘을 잠시 올려다보았습니다
차의 향취를 느끼며
나의 조형다병은 조각가 쇼우선생에게
받은 영향의 자국이 길이 되었을 때
땅을 잠시 내려다보았습니다
어느 한 점에서
조형의 세계가 좁아져가는 듯하는 몸부림이
탑이 되었을 때
흙은 확실하다는 걸 알았습니다
무작정 만든 다병으로 도예가가 되었을 때
한편의 불확실한 것에 매듭조차 없으면
믿음도 없다는 걸 알았습니다
흙에 파묻히는 자세란
얼마나 치밀한 작정인지
이렇게 흙에 파묻히는 자세로 구하는 일에
현대를 사는 인간에서
인간과 같은 원추형의 다병이
창조적인 자기 세계로 살아갈 일에
무작정 나는 겸허해졌습니다

Modern Humans

I praised the aesthetic beauty of the flower and

Looked up at the sky,

Intoxicated with the beauty of nature.

Feeling the smell of tea,

I looked down at the ground for a moment,

Thinking that the mark of my tea pot was a road,

Influenced by Mr. Shaw, the sculptor.

When the world of sculpture was shrinking

At one point

And became a tower,

I knew that soil was a sure thing.

When I became a potter with my random making,

I knew that there was no trust

Without a knot in one of the uncertainties.

How meticulous is the attitude

Of being buried in the soil?

As one of the modern people who lives

In this soil-dwelling position,

I've become unceremoniously humbled that

Human-like conical pots will live

With their own creative world.

생의 반려자

흙에는 조상들의 한이 스며 있다
어려서는 어버이에게
시집가서는 남편에게
그리고 늙어서는 아들에게
따라야 한다는 삼종지도에
그들은 인고의 세월을 흙으로 달랬다
가지가 열매 때문에 꺾이지 않을 만큼
솎아 내면
가지가 서늘해지듯이
화신에게 반항할 수 없는 도예의 길
주장하지 않고 관용과 순종만을 믿는
조상의 유산이 아닐까
흙으로 도자기를 빚어내는 순간
태동을 느끼듯
내게 있어서
흙은 생의 반려자이다

Life's Companion

The soil is permeated with the resentment of
our ancestors.
They used to soothe their troubles with the soil,
Following the instruction that they should serve
Their parents as children,
Their husbands after marriage, and
Follow their sons when they grow old.
Just as the branches feel empty when some fruit is
Cut out so that they do not break because of them,
The path of pottery cannot resist the god of fire.
Isn't it a legacy of our ancestors who believe
In tolerance and obedience without claiming anything?
The moment I make pottery out of the soil,
I feel like I'm feeling the baby kick,
To me
Soil is my life's companion.

SANG-OK

SHIM'S

POETRY

PART 4

신들의 이야기
The Story of the Gods

비스크 자기

루이 15세 퐁파도르 시대 후작부인
화려한 의상과 생활용품과 함께
파도와 같이 휘날리는 갈색머리에도
기댈 언덕이 있을까
화려한 의상에게도
그녀 생존시에 제작된 연질 도자기에게도
쉴 집이 있을까
비스크 자기에게도
휘날리는 갈색머리에게도
놀이터가 있을까
퐁파도르 부인에게도
후작부인 초상에게도
옛길이 있을까
장식 벽화에게도
나에게도 다음 정거장이 있을까
로코코 사람에게도
로코코양식의 도자기에게도
다채로운 색채가 되었을까
유약의 빛은 우아함을
가질 수 있을까
후작부인 같이 그렇게

Bisque

Does the Marquis of Pompadour during Louis XV
Have a hill to lean on,
Even though she flaps her brown hair like waves
With colorful costumes and daily necessities?
Is there a place for her fancy dress, or
For her time-made soft ceramics
To rest?
Is there a playground
For the bisque, or
For her flapping brown hair?
Is there an old road
To the Marquis of Pompadour, or
To her portrait?
Will there be a next stop
For the decorative mural, or
For me?
Would it have been the varied color
For the Rococo people, or
For the Rococo-style pottery?
Can the glaze have grace,
Like the Marquis?

강화의 여걸

단군이 개국 당시 지상에서
중심의 핵으로 표시하여 놓았다
어제는
감사의 제천祭天을 올렸다고
오늘은
바위벽에 부딪쳐 들리는
묘한 울림이
어제보다 나은 오늘이
나와 함께 회오리바람 되자고 한다
어제는
어머니의 사랑이
생명수와 같이
끊이지 않고 흐른다고
오늘은
보다 나은 내일 앞에
갖가지 괴석들이 막아선다
칡덩굴이 엉켜 험난하기만 하지만
내일처럼 살라고
산세의 수려함 보란 듯 살라고 한다
아주 오랜 시간이 흐른 다음
이곳에서 강화의 여걸

수필가 조경희를 기린다고 한다
조경희수필문학관 사이로
나를 끌어당기리
언젠가 미풍이 나를 흔들었던 적 있다

A Heroine of Ganghwado Island

When Dangun opened this country,
He marked it as the core of the center.
Yesterday,
The strange sound of a rock wall
Offered a thank-you service to the sky,
Today,
It is telling me to be a whirlwind together
For a better day than yesterday.
Yesterday, the mother's love
Continued to flow like a lifeline,
Today,
There are various bizarre rocks
Ahead of a better tomorrow.
Even if the road is rough
Due to tangled arrowroot vines,
It seems to be heard that
You should live like tomorrow and
Live as well as the beauty of the mountains.
After a long time
I heard that Cho Kyung-hee,
A female hero essayist from Ganghwado Island,

Will be honored here.

Cho Kyung-hee's Literature Museum

Will attract me.

There was a time when the breeze here shook me.

빛의 흐름 속에

흙이 가지고 있는 가능성
그 잠재력이 순수한 마음에 닿을 수 있고
물살을 헤쳐 헤엄을 치듯이
새로운 형태의 조형물이 탄생한다
빛의 흐름 속에 전개된 다병
페달을 밟아 자전거를 타듯
그림으로 그리거나 형상으로
명멸하는 진실을 건져 낸다
새들이 날개 하나로
하늘을 나는데
다병은 디자인에서부터 갈라진 부분
나의 마음을 움직이게 한다
종심의 나이에도
왼쪽을 둘러보고 오른쪽을 돌아보듯이
불교의 선禪 사상과 결부하고
의식을 불가사의로 끌어 올린다

In the Stream of Light

Earth with possibilities and potential

Is born as a new form of sculpture,

As if swimming through the water

Into a pure heart.

Just like pedaling a bicycle,

A tea bottle is painted or shaped

In the flow of light and

Saves the dying truth.

Birds fly in the sky

With only wings,

This is divided from the design

That moves my mind.

Even at the age of 70,

I look left and look right.

But this,

In conjunction with Buddhist Zen idea,

Raises awareness mysteriously.

카프리 섬

이탈리아 쏘렌토 항에서 페리 고속선을
타고 카프리 섬에 내렸다
수많은 예술가들과 사상가들 중
고르기와 아다네그리가 살았다기에
아름답고 존엄한 느낌을 안겨준다
자꾸 무언가를 주어야 풍요롭게 만든다기에
나는 자꾸 영적인 것을 느끼게 했더랬다
그래도 균형 잡힌 산기슭에
성스러움이 더 많이 생겼다
내가 더 좋아하는 친화성은
도예품에 담고 싶은 모양이기에
거기에 물질과 정신이
자꾸 연결되어
도자기를 만들었던 모양이다
아무래도 그동안 내가
자연 속에서 불가사의를 드러내
상징적인 작품을 만들었는지도 모른다

Capri Island

I got off at Capri Island

By ferry express from Port Sorento, Italy.

Of all the artists and thinkers,

Especially since Gorgi and Adanegri lived here,

It seems that this place is beautiful and dignified.

I kept trying to give a spiritual feeling because

It is said that giving something often makes you rich.

At the foot of the mountain,

I felt a greater sense of sanctity.

My favorite affinity seems to be something

I want to put in pottery.

In addition, the material and spirit are

Constantly connected,

Giving me an incentive to make pottery.

Maybe I've been

Making symbolic works

Through the wonders revealed by nature.

신들의 이야기

12세기경 목마로 유명한
트로이전쟁을 기록한 이곳
신화로 시작하여 많은 상을 만들었다
그리스 역사는 신들의 이야기 그 자체다
수호신인 여신이 있는 아테네신전
원추를 직사각형으로 배치한 도리아식
세부를 고안하여 시각적 조화를 이룬다
중앙 약간 완만한 수평선
넘어질 듯하면서도
결코 걸음을 멈추지 않는
걸어가는 사람처럼
위로 올라감에 따라 가늘고 안쪽으로 기울어진 원추
그대로 신들의 이야기로 이루고
품고 있던 열망을 전해주는 듯
한 측면만으로 나타내지 않는다
그 비너스상은 미와 영원을 이룩한
최고의 이데아를 실현하였다
다른 곳을 닿기 위해
두 다리로 저어가는
한 세상의 신들

The Story of the Gods

This place recorded the Trojan War,

Which was famous for its wooden horse,

Around the 12th century,

It started with myths and made statues of many gods.

Greek history is the story of the gods itself.

The Athenian temple,

Which was built for the guardian goddess,

Is a Doric rectangular building with circular columns and

Detailed designs that are in visual harmony.

The center is a slightly gentle horizon and

Conical columns that lean inwards

As they ascend like a walking person

Who is likely to fall down but never stops walking.

The building itself consists of the stories of the gods,

And does not represent the aspirations of the gods

Only on one side.

This statue of Venus realized the best Idea

That achieved beauty and eternity.

The gods of the world

Are stirring on both legs

To reach another place.

자연의 소리

행복과 불행이 교차하는 삶
희로애락의 굴레를 벗어나지 못한다
산 아래 펼쳐진 평야에 강이 흐른다
흰 눈이 덮인 산들이
사방으로 둘러져 장엄한 풍경이다
나는 매일 나 자신을
만들어야 한다고 외친 사람들 속에서
만년설로 뒤덮인 산에서
하늘을 찌르는 돌산들이 펼쳐지는데
지나온 삶을 돌아보며
밀려오는 슬픔 이기려고
마음의 맷집을 키운 사람이 있다
그 아래
푸른 침엽수 삼나무들
산 전체가 검게 보인다
아득히 먼
하늘을 향해 뻗은 백양나무들
그림자 밟지 않으려고
햇빛 마주보며 걸어가는 나
바람에 나부끼는 쭉 뻗은 나무들
호수 위에 하늘을 인 산들

구름을 수놓고
수십 폭의 병풍처럼 깎아질러 서 있다
내가 만약
나라는 것을 조금이라도 안다면
그건 분명 자연의 소리 때문이다

The Sound of Nature

A life of mixed happiness and misery
Cannot escape the yoke of them.
The river flows through the plain under the mountain
And white snow-covered mountains
Are surrounded in all directions.
Watching the snow-covered
And rocky mountains piercing the sky
In the midst of those who call for
Their own creation every day,
I look back on my past
And think of a man who raised endurance
To overcome his surging sorrow.
Beneath it,
The whole mountain looks black
With the green coniferous cedars.
I walk face to face with the sun
To avoid stepping on the shadows of
Those trees that extend
Far into the sky.
Straight trees fluttering in the wind,
Reflecting on the lake,

Embroidered by clouds,

Are as steep as a folding screen like a dozen.

If I knew

Anything about me,

It's definitely because of the sound of nature.

자화상 앞에서

대만 서양화가가 그린
나의 초상화를 바라보니
젊을 때의 얼굴이 보이고
좋은 인연이 올 것만 같고
가슴에 비 내려도
말없는 언어를 지을 것만 같고
사람의 마음을 품속으로
끌어들이지 않을 때
세상은 불완전하기에
풍요롭다는 말 생각하네
깨달음의 바탕이
인간 밖에 있는 것처럼
생각되는 것 같아
모든 것이 그 속에
있는 것 같기만 하다
세상을 읽어내는 방식으로 생각하네
이것이
경쟁심이 끼어들 수 없는 방식
나의 자화상 앞에서
너를 따뜻한 정으로 품어내는 힘으로
다시 살아간다

In Front of My Self-portrait

Looking at my portrait

Painted by a Taiwanese artist,

I can see the face of my youth.

I have a feeling that I will meet a good relation, and

I feel like I'm able to build a silent language

Even if it rains on my chest.

I think it's rich

Because the world is incomplete

If you don't bring a man's mind

Into your arms.

Everything seems to be in there,

As if the foundation of enlightenment is

Outside of human beings.

I think of the way I read the world.

This is

A way in which competition cannot intervene.

In front of my self-portrait

I live again with the power

To embrace you with warm affection.

잃어버린 꿈을 위하여

8월의 하늘에는
태양이 이글거리지만
산과 들에는 활기가 가득 차 있다
웨지우드의 쟈스파 도예품
꿈 얻지 못한 네 영혼이
불꽃이 되어 내 몸속에 들어와
화신이 되었구나
언제부터 너는
자기에 가까운 반투명의 흰 동체
그 위에 코발트로 착색되었구나
거의 흑색에 가까운
짙은 남색 바탕 위에
유백색 불투명한 유리에
카메오 기법으로 하고
고대 신화가 부조되는 이유를 알았느냐
나도 한때
목 부분부터 어깨 부분의 삶을
그리스 앙포라형도 있었다면
나는 그만
신화로 만든 카메오 기법이
유리 항아리에 장식하고

가마 속에 쉬는 이유를 알아버렸네
오늘은 잃어버린 꿈을 위하여
참다 참다 터지는 울음처럼
전진하는 변화를 추구하고야 말겠구나

For the Lost Dream

In the sky of August,

The sun is blazing,

The mountains and fields are full of vitality.

Wedgewood Jasper Ware,

You became a firework of your soul

That was not been given a dream and

Has come into my body and

Become the god of fire.

Since when have you been

Painted cobalt on a translucent white body

Close to pottery?

Did you know why

Ancient myths were engraved

By Cameo techniques

On a milky opaque glass with a near-black, dark blue base?

Once my life

From the neck to the shoulders

Knew the Greek Amphora,

I would have known

Why the mythical Cameo techniques

Were decorated in glass jars and

Rested in kilns.

Today, for the lost dream,

Like crying out of patience,

I'm going to pursue a forward change.

샌드위치 세대

나는 아직도
전통적인 가치관과 신세대의
핵가족 사이에 놓여있습니다
앞 세대는 고통을 참아내려 하고
뒷 세대는 서슴없이
자기 자신을 표현합니다
마음속에 세운 여성의 가사와 육아에만
쏟아 부었던 생활
세월이 흘러 자기 이익만 찾습니다
생의 다음 페이지를
두려움 없이 넘으려 합니다
그들은 저돌성과 적극성을 꿈꾸었지요
우리는 모두
샌드위치에 있는 남성들도
가정과 사회에서 인정을 필요하니
내일부터는 사회적으로 성공적인 사람이 되자고
페이지를 넘깁니다
부인의 외모와 행동 속에 있는 단순 내조만으로
부족한 시대
나는 이 세대를 위해 살아가고 있습니다
당신이 이 세대를

유일한 샌드위치 세대라 부를 때까지
느티나무 아래서
허망한 세월에 묻히기 일쑤입니다
오직 나는
이 세대를 향해 살아가고 있습니다

Sandwich Generation

I'm still
Between traditional values and
The nuclear family of the new generation.
The previous generation tried to put up with the pain, and
The latter generation express themselves without hesitation.
If there was something in the former's life that
they spent on the housework and rearing children,
After many years,
The latter's life is about pursuing their own interests and
Going beyond the next page of their life without fear.
They dream of being reckless and aggressive.
The men
In our sandwiches need to be recognized
At home and in society,
And they turn the page from tomorrow
To be socially successful.
It's a time when simple assistance
Through your appearance and
Behavior is not enough.
I am living for this generation,
Until you call this generation

The only sandwich generation.

I often see people wasting their time

Under the zelkova trees.

However, I

Am living for this generation.

도시의 그림자

오래전부터 일본인들은 우리나라의 막사발을
이도다완井戶茶碗으로 대접했는데
태토가 빚어낸 진귀함마저 있어서
요즈음같이 물질이 풍부한 시대에
그리워졌는지 모른다
자연과 인간의 끝없는 관계를 유지하는
신비함에 중점을 둔 도시의 그림자
디자인의 언밸런스에서 창의적 조형이다
잠을 막기 위해 은행잎을 달여 먹는
스님도 있다는데
다병의 성형도
틀에 박힌 형태의 되풀이가 아니다
대담하고 기발한 성형방법에
코일로 말아 올린 손작업인데
형태를 누르고 구부려서
점토를 붙이는 변형도
시도 하였다는데
흙 빚으며 나는 무엇으로 사나
이도다완이라고
불리는 산청점토도
속은 찝찔한 눈물 같은 물로

가득차 있고
철광석의 가루도
그린 후에
유약으로 시유도 하였는데
불가마 앞에 앉은 나는 무엇으로 사나
파괴함으로 나는 만든다
그것이 나의 마음도
휘어잡는다

The Shadow of City

A long time ago,

The Japanese treated our Korean bowls

As precious teacups.

Now the material-rich times

Seem to miss them

Containing the rarity created by raw clay.

The shadow of city focused on the mystery of

Maintaining the endless relationship

Between nature and man:

It is a creative formulation in the unbalance of design.

Like some monks

Who drink boiled ginkgo leaf water to prevent sleep,

You shouldn't repeat the shape of the tea bottle

In a conventional form.

Some are trying to roll the clay up into coils

To make bold and ingenious shapes using their hands.

Some are trying to make their own variations,

Pushing the shape, bending it, and attaching the clay to it.

How can I make earth?

Sancheong clay,

Which was used to make precious teacups,

Is filled with tear-like salty water.

Magnetite is also

Used as a glaze

On ceramic paintings.

What do I live for,

Sitting in front of the kiln?

By destruction, I make something

That holds my heart.

SANG-OK

SHIM'S

POETRY

PART 5

일상속의 날카로움
The Sharpness of
Daily Life

대리석 산 일기

대중臺中에 있는 화련花蓮
대만 동부의 중요한 도시
횡귀공로橫貴公路,
소화공로蘇花公路 통과하네
사방으로 에워싸인 대리석이
절정을 이루는데
계곡은 그 자리 그대로 있는데
아리따운 아가씨가 주머니를 얹은 쟁반
따끈한 향편차를 따라주네
오른편은 급한 절벽이고
왼편은 바다가 펼쳐져 있는데
나는 잠자리처럼
이 자리 저 자리 옮겨 다니네
대리석의 장관은 앞을 다투지 않는데
신비스런 경치는 다투면서도 흐르지 못하네
중국대륙문화는 그대로
그것보다 더 섬세한 세공업까지
동시에 볼 수 있을까
다양한 음식보다 더
반복되는 절경이 있을까

아무려면 자연에 감사하면
내가 바라보는 자연
대리석이 둘러싸인 곁에 갈대는
사방으로 에워싸인 나만의 것

A Diary of Marble Gorge

Running Cross-Island Highway and

Suhua Highway

I arrived at Hualian in Taichung,

An important city in eastern Taiwan,

The gorge,

Which is surrounded by marble in all directions,

Forms a magnificent view, and

A beautiful lady gives me

A hot, fragrant flower tea.

There's an urgent cliff on the right, and

There's an ocean on the left, and

I'm free to move both places

Like a dragonfly.

The marbles' magnificent views are not in contention,

But the mysterious scenery

in a state of contention is not flowing.

Can Chinese continental culture be seen

At the same time,

Even more delicate than that?

Is there a more diverse and

Beautiful view than various foods?

Well, thanking the nature that I see,

I am satisfied that the reeds

Next to the surrounding marble

Belong to me.

가을 이야기 속으로

어느 유곡에서 쓰러진 갈대
뒤엉켜 있는 모습이
도예작품의 창조과정에 나타나면
도자기의 다채로운 색채와
유약의 빛은 의아하게 보이던
바다 위 낮달
갈대 소리와 물새 소리의
가을 이야기 속으로 먼저
옮겨 놓은 색채들
식기, 꽃병, 인형에 이르기까지
자꾸 내게로 오는구나
그 시절 목가적인 꿈을
더해 우아하였던 때가

Into the Fall Story

When the fallen and tangled reeds

In a deep valley

Enter the process of creating pottery,

The various colors and glaze of pottery

Become a mysterious day moon

Floating in the sea.

The colors that first moved

Into the autumn story

Of reeds and water birds

Keep coming to me,

From tableware, vases, and dolls:

The days when it was elegant

With idyllic dreams.

오죽烏竹

오죽헌에는 오죽이 하늘을 찌를 듯
온 뜰이 대숲으로 울창일 때
오죽 잎이 세월을 이은 듯
내가 겨울나무처럼
마른 가지일 때
바람 소리마저 신비감을 자아낸다
긴 겨울을 이긴 오죽들은 나에게
겁 없던 말 쓸어 담을 때
자연의 정감을 가져다준다
봄가을 없이
사임당의 어머니가 태어났을 때
다시 사임당과 율곡이 오죽으로
생명의 젖줄 삼아 성장할 때
순이 돋아 오르며
시련과 의지 그리고 지조가 함께 자란다
유교의 실학사상을 기반으로
쓸어 담을 주머니가 없이
새로운 조류가 정립될 때
그 소박성이 미적 안목으로
성장하게 한 그 말
그 까닭을 알 듯하여

Black Bamboo

In Ojukheon, all the gardens are filled
With soaring black bamboos.
Even the sound of the wind from their leaves
That has continued throughout the years
Creates a sense of mystery,
When I feel like a dry branch from a winter tree.
The black bamboos that have survived the long winter
Will bring me a sense of warmth
When I sweep up the words I spit out without fear,
Regardless of season
When Saimdang's mother was born,
When Saimdang and Yulgok grew up
Using black bamboo as the lifeline,
They would have sprung up,
The trials, the will, and the fidelity
Would have grown together.
I think I know the meaning of the simple words
That led to the development of aesthetic insight
When new trends based on Confucianism's practical ideas
Were established so that
There were not enough pockets to sweep.

생각의 눈

인파가 구름처럼 몰려드는
시카고 밀레니엄 공원에 설치된
아니쉬 카푸어 조각 광장
공원 한복판의 이 '구름문'에
빛을 반사하는 거울처럼
이 세상 어딘가에
빛을 반사하는 거울이 있다면
그것은 나를 위한 생각의 눈일 거다
커다란 강낭콩 모양의 구름문에
비치는 상들은 나를 비추지 않는다
블록렌즈와 오목렌즈에 비친 다양한 모습들은
변화무쌍한 영혼을 일깨워 줄 것이다
이 세상 반구 어느 곳에 가까이 갈 수 있다면
세상은 거꾸로 보일 것이다
하늘과 구름을 담고 있는 사람이 있다면
현실과 미지의 세계에 걸쳐 있는 것이다
이런 탐닉에 빠져 있기보다
나는 우리의 생명을 위해 희생할 것이다
보는 각도에 따라 다른 형태로 일그러지기보다
나는 또 다른 세상으로 인도할 것이다

The Eye of Thought

Anish Kapoor's sculpture in Millennium Park, Chicago,
Attracts crowds like clouds.
Like the mirror reflecting the light on the sculpture,
Cloud Gate in the middle of the park,
If there's a mirror somewhere in the world
That reflects light,
It would be the eye of thought for me.
The images on the Cloud Gate
In the shape of a large kidney bean
Don't shine on me.
The various images reflected on the block lens and
Concave lens will awaken the ever-changing souls.
If you could get close to the hemisphere of the world,
The world will look upside down.
If anyone has the sky and the clouds,
He stands with one leg in reality
And the other in the unknown.
Instead of indulging in these thoughts,
I will dedicate myself to our lives.
Rather than being distorted by different angles,
I will try to lead to another world.

어느 도예가의 말

도예는 음악이나 무용보다
자연과 가까운 관계라고 했을 때
과거와 미래에서 현재 서 있는
자신의 실재만이 도道일까 하는 물음으로
헤렌드 요장의 창시자 예노파르카슈하지는
전통방식에 새로운 양식을 추가한
헝가리의 제품을 만들었다
이는 예리한 칼로 섬세하게 도려내는 투각법이다
세공법에 의해 나비들이 그려진 점토를
실타래처럼 만들었는데
그것은 꽃과 과일로 형태를 짜 올라가는 동양적 기법이다
이미지는 표면 안쪽으로 넓어져 강처럼 변해 갈 즈음
화신 때문에 속이 훤히 들여다보이는 사람들에게
나는 상처가 고통이라고 말했지만
나이가 들면서 마침내는
그 상처들이 축복처럼 느껴졌다
불꽃이 방황하고 있는데도
잠재적인 세계와
순수한 마음이 부딪혔다는
어느 도예가의 말을 보태는 밤

A Potter's Remark

When Jeno Farkashazy, who revived Herend pottery,
Heard that pottery was closer
To nature than music or dance,
He questioned whether his real existence in the past
And future was reasonable,
Then he created a unique Hungarian product
That added a new style to the traditional way.
Herend's technique is a delicate method
Of cutting with a sharp knife.
The way to make clay with butterflies on it like skeins is
The same as the oriental technique of
Building up the form of flowers and fruits.
As the image broadens inside the surface,
It becomes like a river.
To the people who are seen because of the god of fire
I once said my wounds were pain,
As I grew older, the wounds finally felt like a blessing.
Even though the flames were shaking,
It's a night when I agree with a potter who said that
A potential world and
A pure heart are connected.

도자기 인형을 찾아서

야드로에서 만든 도자기인형에서
현대적인 감각으로 최대한 늘인 것 같은
얼굴과 몸일지라도
유명한 조각가들의 핸드메이드이다
언제나 도자기를 승화시킨 인형들이라도
늘 혹은 때때로
야드로 삼 형제는
자신의 집에 가마를 쌓아서
도자기를 만들기 시작한 형제들이다
각자도생의 인형들
언제나 희미한 색채일지라도
늘 혹은 때때로
인간과 자연의 모습을 완벽하게
표현해주는 인형이다
날마다
부드러운 파스텔 색조로 만든 인형일지라도
우아한 아름다움이라는 생각
작품마다 표정이라는 생각
이것이 공포와 침묵이다
각자도생의 사랑과 희망일지라도
늘 혹은 때때로

부드러운 표정에서
희미한 색채는 제품 생산이 끝나면
원형을 없애버린다
이것이 구입한 사람들로
인형을 갖게 한 야드로 삼형제

In Search of Pottery Dolls

The pottery dolls made by Llardro are handmade

By famous craftsmen,

Even with their faces and bodies

That seem to have been stretched

As much as possible with modern sensibilities.

The three brothers of the Llardro family

Built a kiln in their house and

Started making pottery.

Even though each living doll

Has a faint color,

They always or sometimes

Perfectly represent

Humans and nature.

Day by day,

The idea that the dolls made of soft pastel colors

Are elegant beauty,

The idea that each piece has a facial expression, and

Perhaps an expression of fear of silence.

Always or sometimes

A soft look,

Even if it's the love and hope of their own lives.

After one work is produced,

They remove the original form.

It's their own craftsmanship

That makes people

Keep the Llardro doll.

철조망 그 너머에

동해 뱃길로 금강산에 갔다
무겁게 가라앉은 잿빛 항구
검게 녹슨 북한 어선에
쭈그려 앉은 무채색 어부들
주위가 온통 회색빛이다
조금씩 금강산 가는
배는 흔들렸다
조금씩 마음도 흔들렸다
나무토막처럼 굳은 표정도
언제나 흔들렸다
철조망 그 너머에
온정리 마을이 보였다
마을을 에워싼 민둥산에 흔들리고
헐벗은 논에 흔들렸다
호기심과 묘한 경계심이 뒤얽힌 시선
단단히 붙들기 위해
만물상과 나는
마주 서있다
나는 거대하게 누워 있는
하얀 암반 속으로
걸어 들어간다

온 세상을 품에 안아버릴 듯한
기세에도
앞으로 나아간다
동산만한 바위에
'자력갱생'이란
붉은 글씨을 흔들리면서
마주 볼 수 있을까
왜 세상은
물질적 빈곤에 흔들리는가

Beyond the Barbed Wire

I'm going to Mt. Keumgang on along the East Sea route.

The gray harbor is heavily sunk.

Achromatic fishermen are squatting

Inside a darkly rusted North Korean fishing boat.

It's gray all around.

When the ship I was riding in shook,

My heart shook little by little.

And their facial expressions,

As hard as a piece of wood,

Soon shook.

Beyond the barbed wire,

I could see Onjeong-ri village.

I was shaken by the barren hills surrounding the village

And by the bare rice paddies.

I'm standing face to face

With Manmullsang

To secure their gaze,

Which is intertwined with

Curiosity and strange vigilance.

I walk into a huge white bedrock.

I move forward

With a force

That will hold the whole world

In my arms.

Can you face the red letters

SELF EFFORT

Carved on a rock

As big as a hill?

Why is the world shaken

By material poverty?

은하의 물빛

콰이강의 다리를 둘러싼
은하의 물빛을 내려다본다
낡고 초라한 다리에 내려갈까 생각 끝에
포로들에 일본군들의 갖가지 만행 떠오른다
밭을 지나 왼쪽으로
내려갈까 생각 끝에
속도를 내기 시작하는 것도
절벽이 나타났다
포로들이 맨손으로 땅을 파고
바위를 폭파하는 것이
버팀목과 레일을 깔았다고 하는 것도
피와 울분이 스며있는 운하도
총을 겨누며 닥치던 일본군들에
마구 짓밟히던 소리도
퍼져 나오는 것이라 생각해 본다
바람이 무심히
흘러가고 만 것도
나쁘지만은 않을 것이라 생각해 본다
활화산처럼 내부로부터 분출을
지키지 못한 탓이다

Galaxy Water Light

I look down at the galaxy water light

Surrounding the bridge on the River Kwai.

Thinking about going down the old, shabby bridge,

I remembered the atrocities of the Japanese soldiers

Against the prisoners.

After that I changed my mind

And went through the field and

Down the river to the left,

And I picked up the pace,

A cliff appeared.

The canal is infused with blood and anger

That the prisoners had vomited

While digging with their bare hands,

Blowing up rocks, and

Laying supports and rails,

And the sound of being trampled by the Japanese military

Is also heard.

I don't think it's a bad idea for

The wind to flow

Inadvertently,

Not preventing active volcanoes from within.

일상속의 날카로움

훈훈한 바람이 불어오고
망고나무와 사탕수수
하이비스카스 꽃이 혼자일 때
나는 갖가지 색상으로 피고 있다
온갖 텃새들이 무리를 짓고
비명을 지르면서 날고 있다
나는 지금껏 너뿐이야 하고
믿어지는 한 사람을 가지는 것이
그토록 권력을 잃고
절치부심하던 그 순간마다
난초를 치며 자신을 다스리는
대원군의 모습이 떠오르는 것
그에게 난초치기
자기만의 독자적인 세계
더 소중하다는 것을 모르고 살아왔다
권력에 대한 불타오르는 의지
숨긴 채 때를 기다릴 줄 아는 것
모르고 살아왔다
이제야 아는 걸
그때도 알았더라면
권력이 먼저 권력에 귀 기울였으리라

분명코 권력을 두고 시소게임을 벌이는 순간마다
묵향에 취해 있는 그 순간
더 행복했는지
권력에 비길 만한 진실은 없다는 걸
일상 속이 날카롭다는 걸
모르지 않았을 것이다

The Sharpness of Daily Life

In the midst of a warm breeze,
When mango trees, sugarcanes, and
Hibiscus flowers are at their best,
I'm blooming in various colors.
All kinds of sedentary birds are flying
In groups screaming.
Daewongun,
Who ruled himself
By growing orchids
While he lost his power
And was desperate,
Would have lived
Without knowing that
His own world was more precious.
He would not have known
Because of his burning will
To get power,
But if he had known then
What I now knew,
One power would have listened
To the other first.

He wouldn't have known

The sharpness of everyday life

Or that he might be happier

When he was absorbed

In the smell of India ink than when

He was playing seesaw games over power.

명사산鳴沙山

사막은 엷은 황색
점차 짙은 색으로 변하고 말았다
다시 잿빛으로 변하여
고비사막의 변두리로 이어진다
명사산은 뜨거운 햇살에 신기루
실크로드에 대해 말하려다
나는 그만 명사산에 대해 말하고 말았다
뜨거운 모래에 연못이 보인다
초승달 모양으로 연못에 대해 말하려다
그만 산록에 대해 말하고 말았다
뜨거운 목마름에 산록이 보인다
붉은색 노란색 흰색 검은색 초록
오색 모래가 쌓았다
모래산에서 사람이 모래와 부딪치면
울음소리에 대해 말하려다
나는 그만 모래벌에
생매장된 사람에 대해 말하고 말았다
한이 아직도 안 풀린 듯하다
굽이굽이 흐르는 초승달 같은 연못
아름다운 물줄기가 흐른다
명사산은 살기 어렵다는데

내가 이렇게 환상의 세계로 미리 말하는 것은
미지의 세계로 떨어지는 일이다

Mingsha Desert

The pale yellow desert gradually turned dark.
And it turns gray again,
Leading to the outskirts of the Gobi Desert.
Mingsha Desert is a mirage in the hot sun.
I was going to talk about the Silk Road,
But I just mentioned Mingsha.
I can see an oasis in the hot sand.
I was going to talk about the crescent-shaped lake,
But I couldn't help but mention a pediment.
I can see the grass because of my parched thirst.
Red, yellow, white, black, green;
Five-colored sand dunes.
I was going to tell you that
When sand and you bump into each other in the desert,
You can hear someone crying,
But I thought of people buried alive in the sand hill.
I don't think their resentment has been resolved yet.
A beautiful stream flows
Through the crescent lake.
Despite the fact that it's hard for anyone to live
In the Mingsha Desert,

Maybe I'm making it fall into the unknown
By expressing it into the fantasy world.

SANG-OK

SHIM'S

POETRY

심상옥의 시세계

The World of Sang-Ok
Shim's Poetry

길위의 꽃

A Flower on the Road

길 위의 꽃

차 성 환 시인

심상옥 시인은 평생을 함께한 도예와 같이 시詩를 빚어왔다. "나는 평생을/짓고 빚는 것으로/일생을 문질렀다/그 힘을 빌려다/한동안 살고 있는 것이다"(「끈」)라는 고백에서 보듯이, 도자기와 시를 짓는 힘으로 스스로의 삶을 가꾸고 영위해 온 것이다. "삶이 사는 것으로/저를 증명"(「고백록」)하기에 그의 삶 또한 그가 빚은 영롱한 빛깔의 도자기처럼, 그가 지은 내밀한 고백의 시처럼 맑고 투명하다. 그는 이번 시집에서 "나는 일생처럼 기다린다 시여"(「시가 온다」)라는 말을 토해내며 시에 대한 강한 열정과 삶에 대한 결기를 보여주고 있다.

『미안한 저녁이 있다』는 황혼녘 길가에 핀 꽃 한 송이를 떠올리게 한다. 시인은 꽃을 통해 사유하고 꽃을 통해 인생을 배운다. "나팔꽃의 꽃말은 '덧없음'/혹시 내 전 생애가/저런 것은 아니었을까"(「꽃에게 묻다」)라며 자신의 지나온 삶을 반추하고 꽃이 알려주는 삶의 아름다움과 고귀한 가치에 귀를 기울인다. '꽃'은 순수한 자연에 대한 비유가 되기도 하고 지상에 왔다가 사라지는 뭇 생명들의 이름이 되기도 한다. 그는 "소박한 마음으로/한 송이 말 속에서 생각을 얻고/한 그루 사람에게서 사는 법을 배운다//꽃 한 송이 나무 한그루가/가장 좋은 책이란 걸"(「다른 날을 꿈꾸다」) 안다. "세상에 지고 돌아온 날/

마음은 더욱 꽃에게로/가까워지는 듯 했습니다"(「꽃속음」). 그리고 그는 "어떤 희망"을 품은 "야생화 꽃씨들을/햇살 좋은 들판에 심을 것"(「다정한 때가 올 것이다」)이다.

심상옥은 꽃의 시인이다. 지금 우리는 죽음으로 스러질 수밖에 없는 인간 존재의 숙명을 이겨내고 자신의 소멸하는 삶을 있는 그대로 사랑하는 눈부신 꽃 앞에 있다. 이 꽃은 "실패한 뒤에야 희망"(「나쁜 날씨는 없다」)이 떠오르듯이 지난한 인생의 여정을 통해 얻어낸 삶의 진리이다. 이 꽃에 도달하기 위해서는 끊임없이 자신의 삶을 성찰하는 데서 시작해야 한다. "나그네"(「길은 나를 버리고」)와 같이 황량한 길 한복판에 서서 지금까지 걸어온 길을 되돌아보고 앞으로 나아가야 할 길을 가늠하며 자신의 내면을 들여다봐야 한다.

> 침대가 누워 있으니
> 사람들이 눕고
> 의자가 앉아 있으니
> 사람들이 앉는다
> 책상이 서 있으니
> 책들을 꽂고
> 문이 닫혀 있으니
> 연다
> 열고 나가면 바깥
> 바깥은 바람천지
> 발은 바람보다 가볍고
> 마음은 미리 내일로 가는데
> 헤매는 이들이 왜 이리 많은가
>
> 우리의 삶은
> 대체로 타향살이
>
> 끝없이 걸어야 이어지는 길처럼

끊임없이 흐르고
벗어던진 옷처럼 고향은
끝없이 버려져 있다

그래도 수거해가지 못하는
삶이라는 무게

 -「삶이라는 무게」 전문

  현대인의 삶은 무의미하고 일상적인 생활에 함몰되어 있다. 타성에
젖어 아무런 의식 없이 "침대"에 눕고 또 "의자"에 앉는 삶을 좋은
삶이라고 말할 수는 없을 것이다. 어떤 반성도 없이 수동적으로 삶을
연명해가는 우리의 모습. 이를 깨치고 "문" 밖으로 나와 길 위에 설
때 우리는 비로소 스스로를 돌이켜 볼 수 있게 된다. "바깥"의 "바람"
을 맞으면서 시인은 한 가지를 깨닫는다. "고향"으로부터 멀어져가는
것이 바로 "우리의 삶"이라는 것이다. 세상에는 '고향'을 잃고 "헤매
는 이들"로 가득하다. 인간은 누구나 다 자신의 근원적 고향인 어머니
에게서 떨어져 나와 자신의 길을 걸어간다. 태어나는 그 순간부터 "타
향살이"가 시작되는 것이다. 그러기에 "끝없이 걸어야 이어지는" 이
"길"은 "고향"에서 멀어지는 길이면서 동시에 되돌아갈 수 없는 "고
향"을 한없이 그리워하는 길이기도 하다. '고향'이란 자신의 정체성을
지켜주는 근원이자 삶을 지속시킬 수 있도록 하는 원동력이기 때문이
다. 우리는 삶이라는 인생길을 걸어가는 내내 끊임없는 상실을 경험한
다. 「삶이라는 무게」에는 우리를 포근히 감싸주었던 안식처, 가족, 친
구, 사랑하는 사람을 하나둘 뒤로하고 "끝없이" 걸어가야만 하는 인간
의 운명이 오롯이 새겨져 있다. '나'는 이 자리에 서 있게 한 존재의
버팀목이자 근원인 '고향'을 되돌아보며 삶의 무게를 가늠해보는 것이
다. "삶이라는 무게"는 버거울 수밖에 없다. 그러나 아이러니하게도
이 삶이 고통스러울수록 '고향'에 대한 그리움은 간절해진다. 심상옥
시인은 끝없이 걸어야하는 길 위에서 자신의 삶을 성찰한다. 그의 시
에는 '고향'에 대한 그리움과 함께 그 존재의 근원을 되찾으려는 힘이

강하게 작동하고 있다. '나'의 존재가 생생하게 살아 숨 쉬던 공간과 시간을 그리워하는 하는 것이다. 시인은 곧 무언가 그리워하는 힘으로 시를 쓴다.

> 쓰러진 나무등걸에 잎이 피어 무사하였습니다
> 폭풍 지나간 자리에도 살아남아
> 어떤 생명이 소리없이 나부꼈습니다
> 그 여름
> 나무의 낯설게 하기에 놀라
> 나는 그만
> 한줄의 절망을 지워버렸습니다
> 세상 어디를 떠돌더라도
> 내 운명의 주사위를 사랑하였습니다
>
> 그 여름
> 나의 인생 단어는 극복이었습니다
>
>   -「나무의 낯설게 하기」전문

여기 삶의 험난한 세파인 "폭풍"에 견디지 못하고 쓰러진 자가 있다. '나'는 폭풍이 지나고 난 후 쓰러져 죽은 것처럼 보이는 "나무"를 찬찬히 들여다본다. "나무"는 자신의 생을 다 끝낸 것처럼 보이지만 "나무등걸"에 핀 "잎"은 아직 스스로 살아있다는 것을 증명한다. '나'는 죽은 "나무등걸"에 자란 "잎"에서 죽음 속에서 피는 생명의 강인함을 발견한다. 여리고 가냘픈 "잎"이 바람에 소리 없이 나부끼는 것을 보고 "어떤 생명"이 가진 근원적 힘을 깨닫는 것이다. 그것은 삶의 무게에 짓눌려 걸어왔던 자신의 삶에서 "절망"이란 단어를 지워버릴 정도로 강렬한 체험이었나 보다. 시인은 죽음을 이겨내고 삶이 간직한 희망과 그 무한한 가능성을 받아들이고 긍정하는 자세를 배우게 된다. 고향을 떠도는 이 지난한 삶을 포기하지 않고 살아내겠다는 강한 의지를 드러내는 것이다. "절망"을 지우고 "극복"이란 단어로 몸을 돌려

세우는 것은 삶의 희망을 믿기 때문이다. 삶을 사랑하기 때문이다. 그렇기에 우리의 인생길은 도무지 알 수 없고 불가해한 일투성이지만 그 알 수 없는 "운명"에 몸을 맡기고 투신하겠다는 시인의 선언은 깊은 감동을 전해준다.

『미안한 저녁이 있다』에는 자기 존재의 근원으로부터 멀어져가는 인간의 숙명을 받아들이고 자신의 삶을 새로이 개척해나갈 것을 다짐하는 시인의 의지가 담겨 있다. 그는 삶이라는 중력에 짓눌리지 않고 이 삶의 여정을 멈추지 않으면서 자신의 생을 끝까지 완수하려 한다. 이 고해와 같은 삶 속에서 희망과 아름다움을 발견하려는 시인의 발걸음은 결코 멈추지 않을 것이다. 그리고 그가 멈춘 자리마다 생의 아름다움이 꽃핀다.

> 금이 아무리 좋아도
> 자꾸 보면 그렇고
> 꽃이 아무리 좋아도
> 자꾸 보면 지는데
> 내 자식은 아무리
> 보아도 지루하지 않네
>
> 사람꽃처럼 보아도
> 보아도 자꾸 보고 싶다는
> 다 늙은 어머니
> 부모의 사랑에는
> 빈, 부의 차가 없네
>
> 세상에서 가장
> 오래된 잠언이네
>
> -「사람꽃」 전문

진아

초저녁에 초승달이 뜨고
새벽에 그믐달이 뜬다는구나
초승달은 금방 서쪽으로 넘어가버리지만
그믐달은 작정해야만 볼 수 있다는구나

초저녁에서 그믐까지
세상에서 제일 먼 길 아니겠느냐
먼 길 가는 이에게
자연은 편애하지 않는다는구나

보아라 딸아
저 잎의 푸름은 나무의 뿌리 아니냐
땅 속에 있어 보이지 않으나
영원한 생명이라 보이지 않는거지
아름다움은 땅 위에 드러나 있는 나뭇잎 같은 것
적은것 작은 것에 기대어 산다면
꽃을 보다가 울기도 하겠지
세상이 생각대로 되지 않겠지만 생각지도 못한
일이 일어나니까 얼마나 멋지냐
그러니 딸아
네가 나아가는 세상에서
너를 끊임없이 만들거라

끝없이 흘러야 썩지 않는 물처럼
넌 그렇게 끝임없이

　-「끝없이 끊임없이-딸에게」 전문

　자본을 상징하는 "금"과 자연을 상징하는 "꽃"보다 더 귀한 것이
있다. "내 자식"은 "사람꽃"에 비할 수 있는, 보고 또 봐도 보고 싶은
유일한 존재이다. "금"과 "꽃"을 주어도 바꿀 수 없는 소중한 존재이
다. 아마도 "늙은 어머니"가 자식인 '나'를 향한 사랑의 표현이었을

것이다. 자식을 쳐다보기도 아까워하는 "부모의 사랑"이 바로 세상에서 가장 오래된 보편적 가치이다. 이러한 "사랑"을 받고 자란 '나' 또한 얼마나 놀랍고 귀한 존재인가. "부모의 사랑"이 대를 물려 내려오듯이 어느덧 '나'는 자신의 딸을 마주하고 앉아 삶의 깨달음에 대해 이야기한다.

"초승달"이 "그믐달"이 되듯이 달이 차오르고 이우는 자연의 섭리와, "세상에서 제일 먼 길"인 "초저녁에서 그믐까지"의 시간을 견디는 법에 대해 가르친다. 그리고 "나무"를 마음으로 바라보는 눈을 터준다. "잎의 푸름"이 단순히 눈앞에서 손쉽게 이루어진 것이 아니라 곧 가지와 줄기를 지나 "나무의 뿌리"라는, 저 깊은 땅 속의 근원에서부터 비롯되었다는 것을 일러준다. "영원한 생명"은 보이지 않는 곳에 숨어있다. "땅 위에 드러나 있는 나뭇잎"은 "푸름"을 간직하고 있다가 순식간에 시들어버린다. 바로 눈앞에서 영원할 것처럼 현현해있지만 순간 명멸하듯이 사라지는 것이 생명을 가진 존재의 숙명과도 같다. 대자연과 우주의 섭리 속에서 인간들 또한 생과 사를 반복한다. 영원하지 않은 것이기에 그것은 가슴 아프게 슬프고 아름답다. 생의 근원적 슬픔이리라. 그러기에 우리는 "꽃을 보다가 울기도" 할 것이다. "꽃"은 슬프지만 아름다운, 눈부신 생의 이미지이다. '나'는 딸이 이러한 삶의 진실을 간직하고 꿋꿋하게 세상을 헤쳐 나갈 것을 당부한다. 자신의 "뿌리"를 늘 기억하고 스스로의 삶을 사랑하며 앞으로 끊임없이 나아가기를 바라는 것이다. 이처럼 시인은 세상과 사물을 밝히 보는 혜안을 가졌다. 어떤 역경에서도 흔들리지 않고 삶의 소중한 가치를 품고 살아가는 자세를 딸에게 물려주고 싶어 한다. "꽃"이 가진 진정한 아름다움을 깨닫고 스스로 생의 아름다움을 가꾸어나가기를 간절히 기도한다.

심상옥 시인은 '사람'에게서 고귀한 가치를 발견하고 이를 "사람꽃"(「비로소」)이라 부르기도 한다. "우리는 누구나/편지나 사진 기념품같은/소형 박물관을 가지고 있습니다"(「어떤 방식」)라는 말처럼 사람은 모두 지금은 잃어버린, 어떤 소중한 기억을 하나씩을 간직한 채 살아간다. 자신의 정체성을 지켜주고 '고향'의 따듯함을 느끼게 해주는 그 기억이 자본이 지배하는 현대의 삭막한 도시의 삶을 견디게 해주는 것이다. 가슴 속에 품은 '고향'이 바로 사람을 아름답게 만든다. '고향'을 그리워하는 마음이 사람을 빛나게 한다. 시인은 "지는 해를 더 오래 바라보"(「다시 궁금한 내력」)는 "종심從心의 나이"(「천천히」)가 되어 비로소 "사람도 하나의 가치라는 걸"(「비로소」) 깨달은 것이다. 살아오면서 사람들에게 많은 상처도 받았을 것이다. "한동안 나를/참으로/아프게 했던 말들"(「한 동안」)에 힘들어하고 마음을 추스르다가 어느 순간 "뒤돌아보니/사람은 간데없고//눈물 나게 하는/노을만 붉게 남아 있"(「지금 오신다면」)기 때문이다. "누구나 울지 않는 밤은 없"(「노력도 쌓으면 탑이 된다」)다. 그러나 그는 사람에 대한 희망을 잃지 않는다. "사람을 온전히 이해할 수는 없어도/온전히 사랑할 수는 있다는 것을/이제야 알겠네"(「하마터면」)라며 무엇보다도 주위의 "사람을 살펴보는 일"(「살펴보다」)에 열과 성을 다한다. 자신의 삶을 회고하며 "누군가의 눈물을 닦아"준 것이 "이곳에서 잘한 일"(「손수건」)이라 말하고 지금도 매일 "한 사람이라도 도울 수 있게 해주셔서 감사"(「아직은」)하다고 기도한다. "다시 태어나면 나는 나무가 되어 네 그늘이/되고 싶다"(「나무는 악착같이」)는 문장은 사람에 대한 지치지 않는 사랑과 헌신으로 살아온 자만이 쓸 수 있을 것이다. 그에게는 "사람만한 꽃이 없다"(「다시, 3월」).

시인은 '사람꽃'을 간절히 찾아다닌다. 그러나 그가 경험한 "서울"에서의 삶은 "별빛은 불빛에 흩어지고/종소리는 차소리에 깨어지는 하루/나조차도 나를 잃어버리고/너조차 너를 잃어버리는 하루"(「서울에서의 하루」)의 연속이다. 그곳에는 "손목시계를 차고도 허둥대는 우리"(「손목시계」)가 있고 모두들 삶의 소중한 가치들을 잊은 채 살아간다. 사람들과 더불어 살 수 있는 세상은 지금과 같은 곳이 아니다. 시인은 사람이 사람답게 꽃피울 수 있는 세상에 대한 꿈이 있다. 그는 우리 곁에서 사라지는 것들을 향해 눈길을 돌린다.

아른거리던 아지랑이가 사라지고
귀 뚫을 듯 울던 귀뚜라미 소리도 사라졌다
연필로 꾹꾹 눌러쓰던 연애편지 사라지고
이별의 상징이었던 손수건도 사라졌다
해질 무렵 어스름 속에서
아이들을 부르던 어머니의 목소리도 사라지고
평상에 누워 별을 세던 어린 시절도 사라졌다
사라진 것이 그것뿐일까
슬픔도 힘이 되던 청춘이 사라지고
'티끌모아 태산'이라던 옛말도 사라졌다
옛 길은 새 길에 밀려 사라지고
초가집은 아파트에 밀려 사라졌다
순정이나 낭만이란 말 사라지고
기적소리 사라지고 감꽃목걸이도 사라졌다
구멍가게 사라지고 골목이 사라졌다

사라진 것들에 대해
회의하는 힘으로 나는 살아간다

　-「사라진 것들」 전문

　여기 사라진 것들의 목록이 있다. 아지랑이, 귀뚜라미 소리, 연애편
지, 손수건, 어머니의 목소리, 어린 시절, 청춘, 옛말, 옛 길, 초가집,
순정, 낭만, 기적소리, 감꽃목걸이, 구멍가게, 골목. 문명의 속도에 쫓
겨 우리 곁에서 아스라이 사라진 것들. 이 단어들만 나열해도 가슴이
따듯해지고 온기가 돈다. 개개의 단어 뒤에 숨은 사연들을 이루 말할
수 있을까. 가을 밤하늘에 수를 놓은 뭇별을 지켜보는 것처럼 우리의
눈은 깊고 맑아진다. "해질 무렵 어스름 속에서" 조용히 숨 쉬고 있던
감각들이 깨어난다. 저 단어들이 숨 쉬던 때는 "불빛보다 별빛이 밝던
시절//밥이 법이 되던 시절//가난에도 운치가 있던 시절//길동무가

좋으면 먼 길도 가깝던 시절"(「끝나지 않은 시절」)이었다. 그러다 잠시 눈을 돌리자 순식간에 자취도 없이 사라진다. 이 모든 것들은 가볍게 명멸하다가 사라질 운명이다. 그리고 "누구도 알 수 없는 역에서/우리는 모두 기차처럼 떠"(「알 수 없는 역에서」)날 것이다.

이 시의 첫 번째 연에서 반복하던 '사라지다'라는 서술어가 두 번째 연에서 "살아간다"로 바뀌는 것처럼, 어쩌면 우리의 삶이란 상실과 이별의 연속이고 사라지는 것 자체가 살아지는 것일 터이다. 시인은 추억 속에서만 반짝이는 "사라진 것들"이 지금처럼 이렇게 손쉽게 사라져도 되는 것인지 의문을 품고 "회의하는 힘으로 나는 살아간다"고 고백한다. 그 "사라진 것들"을 되살릴 수는 없지만 그것의 가치와 아름다움을 현실에 환기시키는 것이 시인의 임무이자 역할이다. 물질과 자본을 축으로 앞으로 달려 나가는 수레바퀴를 잠시 멈춰 세우고 지난 시절 우리를 빛나게 만들어 주었던 순간들을 떠올려보는 것이다.

심상옥 시인은 근원적 그리움을 불러일으키는 사물들, 그 사라지는 것들에 대한 연민과 사랑으로 삶을 살아간다. 그에게 살아간다는 것은 무언가를 그리워하고 사랑하는 말의 동의어가 된다. 시인에게는 믿음이 있다. 사라진 것들을 다시 불러와 세상을 조금 더 아름답게 만들고자 하는 의지가 있다. 그는 우리가 발 딛고 있는 곳이 사람의 냄새가 나는 세상, 조금 더 살만한 세상이 되기를 소원한다. 우리의 삶을 보듬어주었던 소중한 기억들을 가슴에 품고 그것의 사라짐을 안타까워한다. 심상옥 시인의 시집 『미안한 저녁이 있다』는 귀하고 아름다운 한 송이의 꽃이다. 자본의 "새 길"과 "아파트"에 밀려나 이 세상 어디선가 쪽잠을 자고 있을 이에게 "평상에 누워 별을 세던 어린 시절"(「사라진 것들」)의 꿈을 불어 넣어준다. 그리고 지금과는 다른 세상의 아름다움을 볼 수 있도록 우리의 두 눈을 깨끗이 씻어 준다. 나는, "우리 동네에서 제일 깨끗한 것은/성당의 저 종소리뿐", "우리 마을에서 제일 맑은 것은/여울의 저 물소리뿐"(「누구에 대한 짧은 질문」)이라고 말하는 시인의 마을에 가고 싶다. 그의 가슴 속에서 울리는 저 종소리와 여울물소리가 내 귀를 말갛게 씻어 주리라. "살아있는 것들은/스스로 아름다운 운명을 완성"(「누구에 대한 짧은 질문」)하듯이 그의 시를 통해 우리는 밤새 뒤척이고 좀 더 아름다워질 수 있으리라.

A Flower on the Road

by Cha Sung-Hwan

Poet Sang-Ok Shim has been making pottery and poetry all her life. "All my life / I've been building, making / And rubbing. / I've been living / On that strength for a while." (in "String") As you can see from these confessions, she has developed and maintained her own life with the power to create pottery and poetry. Her life is also clear and transparent, like the brilliant colored pottery she created, as "My life proves me by living." (in "Confessions") She is showing her strong passion for poetry and determination for life, expressing the verse "I wait like a lifetime, poet" (in "The Poem Is Coming").

There Is a Sorry Evening reminds you of a flower blooming on the side of the road at dusk. The poet thinks through flowers and learns life through flowers. "The flower of the morning glory means 'futility' / Maybe that's what / My entire life was like." (in "Ask the Flower") Like this, she reflects on her past life and listens to the beauty and noble values of life that flowers tell her. 'Flower' can be a metaphor for pure nature or the name of all living things that come to the ground and disappear. She learns "With a simple mind / To get thoughts from one word / To live from one person. // A flower and a tree / Is the best book." (in "Dreaming of Another Day") "The day I came back from losing the world / My heart seemed to be getting closer / To the flowers." (in "Flower Thinning") And she will do this. "I will plant / 'Some hopeful wildflower seeds' / In a sunny field." (in "There Will be a Time of Kindness.")

Sang-Ok Shim is a poet of flowers. Now we are in front of a dazzling flower that loves its dying life as it is to overcome the fate of human existence, which is bound to collapse by death. This flower is the truth of life obtained through the journey of a difficult life, just as "hope only after failure" comes. (in "There Is No Bad Weather") To reach this flower, you must start constantly reflecting on your life. You should stand in the middle of a desolate road like "a traveler," (in "The Road Has Abandoned Me") reflect on the path you have taken so far, and look inside yourself, measuring the way you have to go forward.

Because the bed is lying,
You lie there;
Because the chair is sitting,
You sit there;
Because the shelf is standing,
You put the books on it;
Because the door is closed,
You open it.
When you open the door, it's outside,

And it's windy there.
My feet are lighter than the wind, and
My mind goes to tomorrow in advance,
There are people wandering about here and there.

Living away from home,
Our lives.

Like a path that leads to endless walks

In our life that flows endlessly
Our home is deserted like a shirt thrown off.

And yet the weight of life
You can't afford.

   - "The Weight of Life"

Modern people's lives are immersed in meaningless and obvious routines. You can't say that living in a bed and sitting in a chair without any consciousness is a good life. It is our passive way of life without any reflection. It is only when we wake up and come out of the "door" and stand on the road that we can reflect on ourselves. In the "wind" of "outside," the poet realizes one thing. The poet says it is "our life" that moves away from "home." The world is full of people who lose their 'home' and "wander." Every human being walks away from his or her mother, who is his or her native home. From the moment they are born, they begin to live away from home. Therefore, this "road" that "only continues by walking endlessly" is a way of moving away from 'home.' At the same time, it is also the way they miss

it because they cannot return to their 'home' through it.
This is because 'home' is the source of their own identity
and the driving force that allows them to continue their lives.
We experience constant loss throughout our life path of life.
"The Weight of Life" is engraved with the fate of humans who
have to walk "endlessly" leaving behind their resting places,
family, friends, and loved ones that have been tightly
wrapped around them. 'I' measure the weight of life by
looking back at 'home,' the support and source of existence
that has kept me standing here. "The Weight of Life" is
bound to be too much. Ironically, however, the more painful
this life is, the more desperate they are for their 'home.' The
poet reflects on her own life on the endless road. Her poems
are strongly influenced by longing for 'home' and the power
to regain its source of existence. Her poems are strongly
influenced by her longing for her 'home' and her power to
regain the source of her own existence. The existence of 'I'
is to miss the space and time when I lived vividly. In other
words, the poet writes poems with the power to miss
something.

    The leaves from the fallen wooden base are safe.
    Surviving the storm, one life flutters silently.
    That summer,
    I was amazed by the unfamiliarity of the trees,
    And I erased
    That line of despair.
    I loved the dice of my destiny
    Wherever I wandered in the world.

That summer
The word of my life was to overcome.

- "The Unfamiliarity of the Trees"

There's a man who collapsed because he couldn't stand the "storm" of life. 'I' look closely at the "tree" that appears to have collapsed and died after the storm. The "tree" appears to have ended its life, but the "leaf" on the "wooden base" proves to be still alive. 'I' find the strength of life blooming in death from the "leaf" growing in the "wooden base." Seeing the soft, thin "leaf" fluttering silently in the wind, the poet realizes the fundamental power of "one life." It must have been an intense experience that erased the word "despair" from her own life, which she had walked under the weight of her life. She learns to overcome death and accept the hope that life holds, and its infinite possibilities, and take a positive attitude. She shows her strong will to live without giving up on her difficult life, which is wandering away from her hometown. She removes "despair" and turns herself toward the word "overcoming" because she believes in hope in life. That's because she loves life. Therefore, the poet's declaration that she will entrust herself to and devote herself to the unknown "fate" is deeply moving, although our path to life is full of unknown and incomprehensible things.

There is a sorry evening contains the poet's will to accept her own destiny as a human being moving away from the source of her existence and to renew her life. Without being weighed down by the gravity of life, she tries to complete her life to the end without stopping her journey. The poet's steps to discover hope and beauty in this sea of anguish will never stop. And everywhere she stops, the beauty of life blooms.

No matter how good the gold is,
You will get tired of seeing it often.
No matter how good the flowers are,
They'll eventually fall.
No matter how much you look at your son,
You're not bored.

My old mother says
She wants to see her children continually
As if they were human flowers,
There's no gap between rich and poor
In parental love.

It's the oldest maxim
In the world.

   - "Human Flower"

Jina,
The crescent moon rises early in the evening,
The dark moon rises at dawn;
The crescent moon soon moves west,
The dark moon can only be seen, only if you're determined to.

From early evening till dawn,
Isn't that the farthest road in the world?
Nature doesn't favor anyone
Who goes a long way.

Behold, daughter,
Isn't the green of the leaves because of their roots?
Though hidden in the ground,
They're the essence of eternal life.
Beauty is like flowers revealed over the ground.
Living on little things and few things,
You'd cry while you're only looking at the flowers.
There are times when the world doesn't go as you expect,
But how wonderful is it that unexpected thing happens?
So, daughter,
In the world you're moving forward
Make you constant.

Like water that doesn't decay because it continues to flow,
You, do the same, endlessly.

   - "Endlessly, constantly, to My Daughter"

There is something more precious than "gold" which symbolizes capital and "flower" which symbolizes nature. "Your children" can be compared to "human flowers" and are the only beings you want to see, even if you keep looking at them. They are precious beings that you cannot change them for "gold" and "flower." Perhaps it is an expression of my "old mother's love" for her child, "I." It is the "parent's love" that even thinks it is a waste to look at your child, and it is the oldest universal value in the world. How amazing and precious I am, who grew up with this "love." As "parent's love" continues for generations, "I" sit facing my daughter and talk about the realization of life.

Just as "crescent moon" becomes "dark moon," it teaches about the nature of the moon rising and falling, and how to endure the time of "early evening to dawn," the "longest road in the world." And she opens her daughter's eyes to look at the "tree" with her heart. She tells her daughter that the "green of leaves" did not simply come from an easy way in front of her eyes, but from a deep underground source called the "root of the tree" beyond branches and stems. "Eternal life" is hidden out of sight. "Leaves on the upper side of the ground" keep the "green" and wither away in no time. It looks bright as if it will last forever in front of your eyes, but disappearing like a flash is like the fate of a life-bearing being. In the providence of Mother Nature and the universe, humans also repeat life and death. It is heartbreaking sad and beautiful because it is not eternal. Therefore, we will "cry while looking at flowers." "Flower" is an image of a sad but beautiful, dazzling life. 'I' ask my daughter to keep the truth of this life and go through the world firmly. She wants her daughter to always remember her "root" and love her own life and move on constantly. As such, the poet has the insight to see the world and things. She wants to pass on to her daughter the attitude of living with the precious value of life without being swayed by any adversity. She desperately prays for her daughter to realize the true beauty of "flowers" and to cultivate the beauty of life on her own.

Poet Sang-Ok Shim discovered noble values in "human" and is sometimes called "human flower." ("At Last") "We have / a small museum where / anyone can store letters, photographs, souvenirs, etc." ("Some Way") As it says, everyone lives with one precious memory that is now lost.

The memory that protects your identity and makes you feel the warmth of your 'home' is what makes you endure the life of the capital-dominated modern desolate city. The 'home' in the heart makes you beautiful. The heart of longing for 'home' makes you shine. It was not until the poet "looked at the setting sun for a longer time" ("Why I'm Curious Again") and "an age at which she could adapt to the logic of nature"(Slowly") that "she realized that human was also a value."("At Last) She must have been hurt a lot in her life. That's because I struggled with "the words / that really hurt me"("For a While") and / controlled my mind for a while,/ and at one point, "when I look back, / there are no people // and / only the sunset / that makes me cry remains red."("If You Come Now") "There is no night when no one cries."("If You Build up Your Efforts, It Becomes a Tower") But he doesn't lose hope for humans. The poet is enthusiastic about "looking at people" around her("Looking at"), saying, "I can't fully understand people / but I can love them completely."("Roughly") Looking back on her life, she says, "wiping away someone's tears" is "good work here,"("Handkerchief") and even now, she prays every day, "thank you for allowing me to help even one person."("Yet") Her verse, "When I'm born again, I want to be your shadow / as a tree,"("Trees Are Tenacious") can only be written by those who have lived with tireless love and dedication to people. "There are no flowers like humans" ("Again, March").

The poet is eager to find the 'human flower'. However, her life in "Seoul" is a continuation of "a day when the starlight is scattered by the light, / the bell is broken by the sound of a car, / a day when even I lose myself / and you lose yourself." ("One Day in Seoul") There is "us floundering even with a watch on our wrists" ("Wristwatch") and everyone lives forgetting the precious values of life. The world in which she can live with people is not the same place as it is now. The poet has a dream of a world where human flowers bloom. She turns her eyes to the things that disappear around us.

The wavered haze is gone;
The sound of crickets' chirping is gone;
The love letter born down with a pencil is gone;
The handkerchief, a symbol of parting, is gone.
At dusk, the voice of mothers' calling children
Is gone;
Our childhood of lying on the low wooden floor and
Counting the stars is gone, too.
Are they the only ones that have gone?
The youth in which even sadness was the source
of power is gone;
The golden old saying, 'many a little makes much' is gone;
The old road was pushed out by the new road;
The thatched cottage was ousted by the apartment;
The words of pure love and romance are gone;
The train whistle is gone;
The persimmon flower necklace is gone;
The corner shop is gone and the alley disappeared.

I live by the power of skepticism about
What things have gone.

-"Things That Have Disappeared"

Here's a list of things that have disappeared. They include haze, cricket, love letter, handkerchief, mother's voice, childhood, youth, old saying, old road, thatched cottage, pure love, romance, train whistle, persimmon flower necklace, corner shop, and alley. The things that disappeared around us, driven by the speed of civilization. Just listing these words will warm your heart and warm you up. Can you say the stories behind each word? Just as you watch stars embroidered in the autumn night sky, your eyes will be deep and clear. The senses that were quietly breathing "in the dusk" wake up. The time those words breathed was when the starlight was brighter than the light, / when rice became law // when there was a beauty even in poverty // when fellow travelers were good("Unfinished Days"), it was a long way to go." Then when you turn your eyes for a while, it disappears without a trace. All of these things are destined to fade away. And "we'll all leave like a train at an unknown station."(At an Unknown Station)

Just as the phrase "disappear," which was repeated in the first verse of the poem, changes from the second verse to "living," perhaps our lives are a series of losses and separations, and disappearing itself is living. The poet asks whether the "disappeared things," which sparkle only in memory, can disappear this easily like now, and confesses, "I live by the power of skepticism about what things have gone." The "disappeared things" cannot be revived, but it is the poet's mission and role to evoke its value and beauty to reality. It is to pause the wheel that runs forward on the axis of matter and capital and recall the moments that made us shine in the past.

Poet Sang-Ok Shim lives her life with compassion and love for the objects that evoke her fundamental longing. Living for her is a synonym for missing something and loving it. The poet has a certain belief. She has the will to bring back the missing things and make the world a little more beautiful. She hopes that the place we are stepping on will be a world that smells like humans, a world worth living a little better in. She feels sorry for the disappearance of the precious memories that have taken care of our lives in her heart. The poet's collection of poems, *There is a Sorry Evening*, is a precious and beautiful flower. To someone who is sleeping in a small space somewhere in the world("The Disappeared Things"), pushed out by capital's "new road" and "apartment," she brings out her dream of "a childhood when she was lying on the low wooden floor and counting stars."

SANG-OK

SHIM'S

POETRY

 역자 후기

　기원전 암석하나 풍화되어 생성되었을지 모를 흙을 빚어 도자기꽃
으로 형상화하더니
그 꽃들을 다시 시로 피워낸 심상옥 시인의 시꽃들이다.
벌써 3권째 시인의 시들을 번역하는 기회를 가졌다.
그만큼 그만의 독특한 시세계에 더욱 내밀하게 몰입할 수 있었고,
그 속에서 그의 인간미와 순수성 그리고 예술에 대한 열정의 분출을
목격할 수 있었다.
번역가의 기쁨과 보람이 여기 있다.
오랜 동안 감수자로 기꺼이 수고해온 자넬 리브와 이 기쁨, 보람을 함
께 하고자 한다.
늘 이 번역자에게 신뢰를 보여주시는 시인께 감사한다.
아마존 킨들 출판 관계자 및 독자들에게도 감사한다.

2021년 새봄을 기다리며

역자 라이채

The Translator's Note

These are the poetry flowers of poet Sang-Ok Shim, who
created earth that may have been produced by a weathered
rock during the B.C. period, and then made them into
pottery flowers, and bloomed them again in poetry.
I have already had the opportunity to translate the poet's
poetry for the third volume.
I was able to immerse myself more closely in her unique
world of poetry.
In it, I could see her humanity, purity, and passion for art.
Here is the joy and reward for the translator.
I would like to share this joy and worth with Janell Reeve,
who has been willing to work as my proofreader for a long
time.
I thank the poet who always shows me trust as her
translator.
I also thank the Amazon Kindle publisher and readers who
will read these poems.

Waiting for the new spring of 2021

Translator Eechae Ra

시 인 심 상 옥

1945년 일본 도쿄출생
경남여고, 이화여대 사범대학교육학과, 동아대학 교육대학원 졸업.
중국중화학술원위원(예술박사), 일본 草月조형학교(사범 3급 취득).
부산대학, 계명대학, 상명대학, 대만실천전과대학, 중국중앙공예미술대학
강사 역임
1982년 시집「그리고 만남」으로 시 등단
고교시절 유치환 시인으로부터, 이화여대 재학시절에는 이동주 시인으로
부터, 이후는 이봉래 시인으로부터 문학지도를 받음
『한국수필』 조경희선생 추천으로 수필등단(1982년)
국제PEN한국본부 부이사장, 한국시인협회이사 역임
현재 한국현대시인협회 이사, 한국여성문학인회 이사장 역임,
한국문인협회 자문위원, 국제PEN한국본부 주간 역임,
문학시대 기획상임위원, 계간문예작가회 이사
시집:「울림과 색깔의 합주」,「오늘과 내일 사이」,「지금 오는 이시간」,
「그리고 만남」,「미안한 저녁이 있다」, 영어시집「삶이여, 안녕한가?」
「그의 말에 물들 때」,「다시, 기원전」(아마존 킨들 발행) 등 8권
수필집:「공간에 색깔 입히기」,「합주」등 8권
수상: 한국문학상, PEN문학상, 노산문학상, 한국여성문학상,
한국수필문학상, 동포문학상, 허난설헌문학상 등 다수.

이메일: sangokshim@hanmail.net
다음 블로그: http//blog.daum.net/sangokshim
네이버 블로그: http//blog.naver.com/sangokshim

Poet Sang-Ok Shim

She was born in Tokyo, Japan in 1945.

She graduated from Kyungnam Girls' High School,
Ewha Women's University, and Dong-A University's Graduate
School of Arts and Education.

She became a member of the Chinese Academy of Sciences
by earning a doctorate in art from it.

She obtained a third-degree master's from the Japanese Plant
and Moon Sculpture School.

She has taught at the Busan University, Keimyung University,
Sangmyung University, Taiwan Shih Chien University, and
China Central Institute of Applied Fine Arts.

She has held 18 pottery exhibitions and 30 domestic and
international group exhibitions.

She was taught literature by poet Yoo Chi-hwan in high
school and poet Lee Dong-joo in her school days at Ewha
Womans University, and poet Lee Bong-rae.

She debuted as an essayist through the *Korean Essays* on the
recommendation of essayist Cho Kyung-hee and as a poet
through "And a Meeting" in 1982.

She is the vice president of Pen International Korea Center,
director of the Korean Modern Poets Association, consultant
of the Korean Writers Association, the planning committee of

the *Literary Era*, and director of the quarterly *Literary Writers Society*.

She was the chairman of the Korean Women's Literary Society and chief editor of the Pen International Korea Center.

Her 8 collections of poems: "The Combination of the Resonance and Color," "Between Today and Tomorrow," "This Time That's Coming," "And a Meeting," "There Is a Sorry Evening," and English collections "Hello, Life," "When I Am Dyed with His Words," "Again, B.C."(Amazon Kindle Edition).

Her 8 collections of essays: "Incarnation," "Beyond the Fantastic World," "After Kindling the Mind," "Playing the Bigger Nature," "Coloring the Space," "Beauty and the Witch," "Ensemble," "To Bloom One Flower."

Her awards: the Korean Literature Prize, the Korean Women's Literature Prize, the PEN Literature Prize, Nosan Literature Prize, the Korean Essays Literature prize, Dong-po Literature Prize, HeoNanSeolHeon Prize, etc.

email: sangokshim@hanmail.net

blog: http//blog.daum.net/sangokshim
　　　http//blog.naver.com/sangokshim

역자 라이채

Translator Eechae Ra

번역문학가. 문예지 "문학 수" 번역위원 및 번역 심사위원.
종합문예지 "한국문인" 편집주간 및 번역책임자 역임.
덕성여대 영어영문과 졸업. 미연방한의사.
「세상의 빛 어머니 사랑」(영역), 「하프 라이프」(국역) 외, 다수의
영한 대역서와 「수필의 끈을 풀다」 외 다수의 공동 작품집이 있다.
한국문인번역문학상 본상 수상.

She is representative translator and on the Translation panel of
Literature magazine *Munhak Su* and served as the managing editor
and translator of the *Korea Writers*.
The United States Diplomate of Oriental Medicine.
B.A., English Language and Literature, Duksung Women's University
of Korea.
She translated "The Light of the World, Mother's Love" (Korean into
English) and "Half Life" (English into Korean), and many other
translation works and has many joint works, including "The
Literature of Filial Love" and "Untie a String of Essays."
She is a Korea Writer's Winner for Excellent Translation.
email: isakok@hanmail.net

Made in the USA
Monee, IL
27 February 2021